MARCEL BREUER AND A COMMITTEE OF TWELVE
PLAN A CHURCH

Marcel Breuer and a Committee of Twelve Plan a Church

A Monastic Memoir

Hilary Thimmesh, OSB

SAINT JOHN'S UNIVERSITY PRESS
COLLEGEVILLE, MINNESOTA

Design by Ann Blattner. Illustrations by Renée Cheng.

1	2	3	4	5	6	7	8

Library of Congress Cataloging-in-Publication Data

Thimmesh, Hilary.
    Marcel Breuer and a Committee of Twelve plan a church :
a monastic memoir / Hilary Thimmesh.
        p.   cm.
    ISBN 978-0-9740992-7-9
    1. St. John's Abbey (Collegeville, Minn.)—History—20th century.
2. Benedictine architecture—Minnesota—Collegeville.   3. Breuer,
Marcel, 1902–1981.   4. Collegeville (Minn.)—Buildings, structures,
etc.   I. Breuer, Marcel, 1902–1981.   II. Title.

NA5235.C6T49   2011
726.509776'47—dc22   2011011734

This book is dedicated to the memory of Baldwin Dworschak, OSB, who as abbot of Saint John's took the long view of Benedictine life and culture as he set about building a house of prayer for our time.

Contents

Introduction

The Saint John's church designed by Marcel Breuer is a monument to the energy and the confidence of the monastic community as we reached our centennial peak half a century ago. The building has been widely recognized for its architectural distinction and the excellence of the craftsmanship that went into making it. Whether it will stand for the ages only time will tell. As we got down to serious talk about building the church, Breuer observed in response to a question that oxidation might weaken reinforced concrete over the long haul. This hadn't happened in the first century of reinforced concrete construction, but whether the combination of steel and concrete would turn out to be as durable as medieval stonework was an open question. The topic came up because Father Cloud Meinberg, himself an architect before joining the community, cited twelfth-century Abbot Suger's decision to renovate the Romanesque church of Saint Denis along the lighter but structurally risky lines of the then new Gothic style. Cloud saw Suger's break with the past as historic precedent for Benedictine risk-taking in church architecture.

Not that a parallel between the medieval abbot and Baldwin Dworschak, abbot of Saint John's from 1950 to 1971, was apparent at first glance. No one expected Baldwin to be a trailblazer. Elected abbot at the age of forty-four, he was the most buttoned-down of superiors. He had served as prior for the last four years of Abbot Alcuin Deutsch's twenty-nine-year reign, and he gave no indication of an adventuresome streak when he reluctantly took office to succeed Alcuin. Nonetheless, four years later he took the lead in approving the revolutionary Breuer design.

In one respect he had little choice. Everybody could see that we had outgrown the 1882 church. There were too many monks to fit into the choir stalls and too many students to fit into the body of the church. Since all indications were that both numbers would continue to grow, no one objected to including a larger church in the comprehensive campus plan Marcel Breuer was commissioned to do in 1953. Reaction to the church that Breuer designed as part of the comprehensive plan was another matter. Could this odd shape be a church? It didn't look like a church. The curious concrete billboard that stood on stiff legs in front of it was a particularly odd and ungainly substitute for a bell tower.

How the community grew accustomed to the design and joined in planning the church and finally built it is the story of this memoir.

Preliminary Planning: 1954–1956

I On a clear summer morning sunlight slants through the ground-level east windows of the church during the psalms of Morning Prayer and glances off the waxed brick floor to cast a pattern of dappled light on the opposite wall. The pleated concrete surface seems to ripple slightly in the morning breeze like the tent to which Marcel Breuer compared the structure when he first presented the church design in 1954.

The slender piers that bear the weight of the side walls and roof of the church encourage this illusion. In Gothic architecture the clerestory admits light through windows high above the side aisles. Breuer brought the clerestory windows down to the floor. The concrete and granite shell of the church seems to rest on panels of clear glass looking out into the cloister gardens. The piers, set at a ninety-degree angle to the axis of the church to minimize their mass, serve as vertical dividers in a glass wall. The end walls of the structure—the three-story north wall of concrete hexagons and the concrete-block south wall behind the organ screen—appear to support the roof but in fact carry only their own weight.

The visual simplicity of this complex structure was central to Marcel Breuer's thinking. Faced with the prospect of doing a monastic church, he found common ground between Bauhaus functionality and the unadorned lines and spaces of historic monastic architecture at its cleanest and sparest. Primitive Cistercian foundations like twelfth-century Senanque in its remote valley east of Avignon come to mind. There the original structures sheltered the monks in spaces defined by unornamented walls, lighted by functional windows with no hint of Gothic tracery. The beauty of this architecture results from the perfect proportion of squared and rounded solids and the interplay of sunlight and shadow on the walls, roofs, and bell tower.

Breuer was commissioned to proceed with working drawings for the new church in December 1956. I was close to this process as a member of the church planning committee from 1956 to 1961. My main qualifications were that I was young enough to represent the junior members of the monastic community and dutiful enough to keep minutes as secretary.

The Architect

The story of how we selected Breuer has often been told. In 1953 I was still studying for the priesthood when Abbot Baldwin Dworschak sent his letter to twelve noted architects inviting them to do a comprehensive plan for Saint John's. I don't know what prompted him to think that architects with national and international reputations might be attracted to Collegeville. Frank Kacmarcik surely suggested some of the architects and perhaps the idea. Frank was then a new member of the art department and owed his appointment to Baldwin in the abbot's role as college president. Several of us had a hand in phrasing the abbot's letter in language designed to interest major architects in doing a comprehensive plan with a bold new church at the heart of it.

Marcel Breuer was one of the architects who responded. He was European, born in Hungary, educated in Vienna and at the Bauhaus in Germany, where he pioneered in the design of tubular steel chairs. He moved to England in the 1930s, then to the United States where he held a position in the newly established Harvard School of Design as a protégé of Walter Gropius, Bauhaus founder. In 1941 he started his own architectural firm in New York. When he responded to the abbot's letter in 1953, he was best known for his furniture designs and private residences. He had just been chosen to design the UNESCO building in Paris.

He came to Saint John's and we liked him. In a way the reason for choosing him to do the comprehensive plan and the buildings that followed was that simple. What was it that made us comfortable with him? He wasn't Catholic. His manner was certainly not midwestern. Later on, people said his humility was appealing, but Bob Gatje, who had a long professional relationship with Breuer, remarks in his full-length study, *Marcel Breuer: A Memoir*, that the architect had a sizable ego, and we monks may have been misled by his manner when he was with us.

I don't think we were wrong about his integrity. From the start he came across as seriously committed to an aesthetic of "good materials sympathetically used," as he put it on one occasion. His manner was customarily measured and thoughtful and on the whole rather formal. We were rarely to see him in shirtsleeves. He and Abbot Baldwin became friends, but it is hard to imagine their small talk; the abbot once observed that Breuer was not the kind of man who flew in from New York and told you about the flight.

Breuer's 1954 comprehensive plan for the campus included the church in the location and the shape it was to have when completed. The new monastery wing had to be built first. Once it was completed in 1955, there was a certain logic to getting on with plans for the church. An unpainted patch on the north side of the new building showed where the church was to be connected. The sacristies for the church were already in place on its basement and first-floor levels. The Breuer wing, as it was later dubbed, jutted out into the front yard of the monastery and spoiled the impressive east front—some 323 feet long—that the first abbots had planned and built in the 1870s and '80s. A wooden stairway meant to be temporary linked it to the Quad, which was slated for demolition in the comprehensive plan.

The Committee

In October 1956 Abbot Baldwin appointed a committee to plan the church, and that is where my story properly begins.

The abbot named a committee of fourteen, all of them monks. Two of them served only briefly. Hubert Dahlheimer was pastor of the Church of Saint Joseph in Saint Joseph and I think attended only the first couple of meetings. Gerald McMahon was appointed chaplain of the Benedictine Sisters of the Villa Sancta Scholastica in Duluth in 1957 and was not replaced. Thus it was a committee of twelve chaired by the abbot which worked with the architect from October 1956 to September 1960, when it ceased to meet.

Four members were chosen for their particular positions. Cloud Meinberg had briefly been a practicing architect before joining the monastery. He taught courses on architecture in the college. He tended to take the long view of contemporary issues, which sometimes irritated people who wanted answers in the present. Nevertheless, his grounding in historic church architecture provided a valuable perspective on contemporary church planning.

Godfrey Diekmann played the oboe in the school orchestra and could have been its director in the grand manner of a Bernstein or a von Karajan. He loved audiences, taught a course on ancient Christian sources that became famous, edited the liturgical monthly *Orate Fratres*, later *Worship*. As Father Virgil Michel's successor in the liturgical movement he was internationally recognized as a spokesperson for liturgical renewal.

Lancelot Atsch was newly appointed pastor of St. John the Baptist Parish, Collegeville. Since the abbey church served as the parish church the pastor was a natural choice for the planning committee. A native New Yorker, Lancelot had a bluff, outgoing personality and was a bit of an operator. His talent for compromise stemmed from a pragmatic outlook on things mundane and spiritual. He taught religion and served as college chaplain before becoming pastor of the Collegeville parish.

Florian Muggli, the monastic "procurator" or treasurer, taught math briefly before Abbot Baldwin appointed him procurator in 1955. He was to hold this position of major responsibility for the rest of Baldwin's tenure as abbot, sixteen years of crucial growth and change in the community which he managed with unfailing attention to detail, patience in dealing with individual monks, and a frugality edifying as a personal trait but trying as a principle of corporate development.

Of the other members, Joachim Watrin taught geometry in the Prep School and for seventeen years designed liturgical symbols for the covers of *Orate Fratres*. Chancy health kept him close to home. He cultivated kinship with nature by walking in the woods and bringing home newborn fawns to be bottle-fed on the back lawn. Jeremy Murphy, lawyer (Harvard College, magna cum laude, 1930; Georgetown Law School, 1934), entered the monastery in 1945, and in 1956 taught political science and served as the immediate superior of the fifty or so junior monks studying for the priesthood.

A group of monks with advanced degrees in their fields and in the early stages of their careers as college teachers gave the committee a strongly academic cast. Colman Barry, American church history, had just finished *Worship and Work*, the centennial history of Saint John's. Like Cloud, he took a historical view, but his view was to the future. He would be a dynamic president of Saint John's University in the '60s. Alfred Deutsch, English, had a warm spot in his heart for human foibles. In later years he would publish two books of slightly fictionalized stories about monks he had known, *Bruised Reeds* and *Still Full of Sap, Still Green*. He had been dean of the Prep School for half a dozen years and now lived among college students as a prefect, tempering his disciplinary role with paternal warmth and a deep-grained sense of Benedictine moderation.

Benedict Avery, classics, and Michael Marx, theology and Scripture, were also academics in the prime of their career, sharp critics, at home in the world of ideas. Benedict had grown

up in New York as a precocious only child who knew from the
age of five that he wanted to be a priest but suppressed any urge
to be emotional about it. Michael had gone to Sant' Anselmo,
the Benedictine college in Rome, in 1938, got a doctorate in
theology in 1943, but because of the war wasn't able to come
home. He made the most of his enforced sojourn by taking an
advanced degree in Sacred Scripture at the Pontifical Biblical
Institute over the next two years. He came home with an Italian accent and joined the faculty in 1945. In 1956 he was also
chaplain to the Convent of Saint Benedict in Saint Joseph. He
and Benedict tended to see eye to eye with Frank Kacmarcik, of
whom more later, in matters of taste and piety.

The subprior, John Eidenschink, chaired the committee in
the abbot's absence and brought to it his perspective as a professor of canon law and master of ceremonies for the abbey. I
was the junior member, ordained two years, teaching English
part-time on the strength of a new MA from Cornell, direct-
ing the college pre-divinity students, presumably representing a
younger generation of twenty or so recently ordained priests and
seventy-seven Clerics and Novices.

Fifty years later I'm struck by the relative youth of this group.
At fifty-five, Gerald McMahon was the only member older than
Breuer at fifty-four. Abbot Baldwin and Fathers Hubert and
Joachim were fifty. Then in descending order came Godfrey
and Jeremy at forty-eight; Lancelot at forty-seven; Michael at
forty-three; Alfred, Cloud, and John all at forty-two; Benedict
at thirty-seven; Colman at thirty-five; Florian at thirty-one; and
me at twenty-eight. We mirrored the average age of the community. In 1956 it was forty; today it is sixty-eight and we are less
tolerant of stairs.

The Community

This was a big committee, so big that meetings with all of the
members present were rare. Nonetheless, what will strike any
reader fifty years later is that no lay brothers, sisters, laymen or

laywomen were included. In part this reflects who we thought the church was for: the monks resident at the abbey; the students—prep, college, and seminary—the latter only occasionally since the new diocesan seminary had its own chapel; employees of the abbey, almost all of them male, including the few lay faculty members; and the Collegeville parish, made up mostly of local farm families. The Franciscan sisters who had the vital function of feeding us three times a day had their own chapel and their own secluded observance. Although Sister Johanna Becker of Saint Ben's was on the art faculty, I don't recall that she or any other woman ever attended a meeting of the committee. For all of the female influence on our thinking we could have been in Macedonia at ancient Mount Athos on its peninsula forbidden to women.

The large elements of parochialism and chauvinism implicit in our communal self-image didn't occur to me then. The composition of the committee simply reflected how we thought about ourselves. The list of Saint John's monks published in the *Ordo*, the annual calendar of liturgical feasts and readings, was divided into four canonical categories: *sacerdotes, fratres clerici, fratres conversi, novitii*, literally *priests, clerical brothers, lay brothers, novices*. In community parlance these were "the Fathers," "the Clerics," "the Brothers," and "the Novices," a nomenclature that we shared with the rest of the American Benedictine world.

Saint John's numbered 333 monks in 1956. Sixty of these were lay brothers. There were also twenty-two novices, half clerical, half lay—some of them in our Puerto Rican and Mexican missions—and five claustral Oblates, laymen living in the community without monastic vows. The number of monks at Saint John's was a fraction of the total, since the abbey staffed more than fifty parishes and chaplaincies and had monks ordained and non-ordained in five distant missions. About forty of the lay brothers were in residence at Saint John's and were in the church several times a day for an English version of the Divine

Office, Mass, and community devotions. Representing them on the committee would have made eminently good sense, most of all when choir seating upstairs and a separate chapel downstairs primarily meant for their use were under discussion.

As for laypeople, one parishioner with young children or an aging parent might have cautioned us not to bury the only restrooms in the church down a flight of twenty-two granite steps in the darkest corner of the basement.

October–November 1956

II The committee met for the first time on October 15, 1956. Abbot Baldwin told us that he had written to Marcel Breuer to say that we were beginning formal study of the church plans. He asked whether Breuer had revised or modified the plans since he originally presented them to us. This was the first of a series of meetings leading up to a chapter vote in mid-December to authorize proceeding with plans. This in turn would lead to Breuer's first meeting with the committee a few days later in the same month. He was to meet with the committee ten times over the next five years.

Our first concern was the novel architecture. We needed assurance that it was all right to build this odd structure and call it a Catholic church. The architect's conceptual design for the church had been floated along with news of Breuer's comprehensive plan in 1954. *Time* noted it in April; *Architectural Forum* published several pages of drawings and favorable commentary in July. Archbishop Brady of Saint Paul was reported to disapprove of it. Bishop Peter Bartholome of Saint Cloud was non-committal. Cloud had devoted a year-long sabbatical to studying church art and architecture in western Europe, including Le Corbusier's church at Ronchamp. He had also consulted influential church figures like Archbishop Luigi Costantini. Colman observed that

Costantini's generally favorable reaction to Breuer's sketches should quell those who objected that the Holy See did not approve of modern art. Cardinal Giacomo Lercaro, mentioned as *papabile* in the waning years of Pius XII, was quoted on the impossibility of asking a modern architect to build in a past style.

Closer to home, the committee noted something less than wholehearted support for the plan in the community. "The outside Fathers" were reported to be down on modern architecture. In matters that came before the Chapter, this body had been a party to be taken seriously ever since the election of the abbot in 1875, when the twenty-four members of the Chapter divided along parish/school lines. In monastic parlance, "outside Fathers" referred to priests stationed in parishes and missions close enough to come home for chapter meetings, annual retreats, funerals, big celebrations. In practice this meant the ones in Minnesota parishes and missions. In 1956 there were about seventy of them scattered among some fifty-five Catholic communities large and small. Whether they all had the same attitude toward modern architecture may be doubted, but Alfred ventured that they were "a vociferous minority" who nonetheless needed to be heard and kept informed. Colman expressed doubt about educating older men but agreed that the committee's proceedings should be entirely open.

Some all too human biases were noted in the community, some against the abbot, some against Breuer as a non-Catholic. Lancelot thought the banner might be the sticking point for in-house critics. John observed that the church plan had lots of theological thinking behind it and that Father Balthasar Fischer, noted German liturgical scholar, had reacted favorably to the plans. Bit by bit we got comfortable with the radical design of the Breuer church and the idea that it could be the new church the community needed.

Two more meetings in early November ranged over Breuer's plusses and minuses as an architect. Having lived in the new wing of the monastery for more than a year, we had our issues.

The fireplace in the Fathers' rec room on the first floor didn't draw properly. The place filled with wood smoke (as distinguished from the blue haze of cigar smoke to which we were accustomed after meals) when somebody tried to get a fire going during the after-supper recreation period. This was particularly gratifying to those who thought fireplaces were an unmonastic extravagance to begin with. The wooden bars on the sliding plate-glass picture windows kept coming unglued. Moral: monasteries shouldn't have picture windows. Also, Breuer was too expensive; everything was custom made. Brother Hubert Schneider at the carpenter shop had to get a special thickness of wood to make the bookshelves that were mounted on the walls in private rooms. And was it true that the perforated metal cans that served as light fixtures in the corridors and rec rooms cost ten dollars apiece?

Ray Hermanson, local architect and alumnus, came to a meeting in the art library on November 6 and dealt with many of these complaints as well as serious questions about the design of the church. Ray was a soft-spoken diplomat whom everyone respected. His influence at this point in the church project should not be underestimated. He was reassuring on individual questions and on the overall quality of Breuer's work. Ray was the quintessential Minnesotan, adept at coming across as the average man concerned to save a buck where possible but also to get his money's worth in a good solid building that would stand up in winter weather. He thought that Saint John's got its money's worth in the new monastery wing, and he was reasonably confident that Breuer could do as well with the church.

Nevertheless, the committee had some questions about engineering and construction. Could we depend on this reinforced concrete shell to age well, or was there a danger of structural cracks over the years that would render the building unsafe or require massive repairs? How do you build such a thing? Would the banner need to be poured in one piece? Wouldn't the formwork be terribly expensive? In our climate was it wise to make the major exposure of the church an immense glass wall facing north?

There were good questions about the difficulty of construction and the relative expense of this singular approach to building a church. Hermanson said that yes, indeed, the European work of Enrico Nervi, Breuer's consultant on structural engineering for this church, was unique. There was nothing like it in this country. That did not mean that this mode of construction was likely to be more expensive than conventional ways of building. Doing an imitation Gothic church would be just as expensive.

In response to questions about the formwork, Ray remarked that the contractor would probably want to have a special man on the job at the start. He had said as much to Breuer and Breuer had agreed. When the time came, "the special man on the job" would be Val Michelson, a Russian-born Twin Cities architect who would leave his own mark on the campus with his design for Saint John's Preparatory School in 1962.

December 13–17, 1956

III The committee got down to business when it met on Thursday, December 13, to consider what figure to put before the monastic Chapter to fund church planning. We used Breuer's rough estimate of cost to come up with a number. The problem was that he had given us two numbers depending on what size church we wanted. How many people did we want the church to seat? We weren't sure. The answer depended on how large we expected the college to get. The church needed to be large enough to accommodate all of the college students who lived on campus, since we still expected them to attend Mass every day.

When we outlined our needs for the comprehensive plan in 1953, we told Breuer we wanted a church that seated 1,250 college students upstairs and about 300 parishioners downstairs. Three years later the September 28, 1956, issue of the school paper, *The Record*, boasted a record college enrollment of 1,002 in a lead article by Al Eisele, a junior destined to go on to a national career in journalism. Continued growth was anticipated. Those were the years when Father Arno Gustin, the dean, egged on by Father Walter Reger, envisioned Saint John's as the Notre Dame of the north. Prompted by his expansionist outlook we asked ourselves whether we should plan a church for 1,650 students rather than 1,250.

These were the alternative numbers on which two ballpark cost estimates for construction were based: $1.2 million or $1.5 million excluding furnishings. The architect's fee would be 8 percent of the total cost. Add mechanical and structural engineering fees for another 2 percent. For the larger church the combined fees would thus add up to nearly $150,000. The committee hashed over these numbers and finally decided to recommend an architect's fee based on plans for the larger structure. At a chapter meeting the next day the abbot requested $112,500 to engage Marcel Breuer to prepare working drawings. The chapter vote was better than 2 to 1 in favor, 72 to 28 with 3 neutral, thus clearing the way to proceed with planning.

Abbot Baldwin estimated that it would take a year to complete working drawings. He got in touch with Breuer immediately, and the architect scheduled a visit for the following Tuesday–Wednesday.

Floor Plan of the Sanctuary and the Choir

Preparing for his visit we had an open meeting on Monday to review questions about the floor plan of the church that had surfaced in a community questionnaire. Most of the questions concerned the altar and the sanctuary. For example, how much higher than the main floor of the church should the sanctuary be? In the typical Catholic church a communion rail was mounted on a step that served as a kneeler and separated the body of the church from the sanctuary. Inside the rail were a lectern or pulpit, seating for priest and servers, one or two small tables, and more steps leading up to the altar. In our present Great Hall, the former church, one can still see evidence of this arrangement. Some of the steps are still there: two where the communion rail was, three more to the upper level of the sanctuary. No longer there are the three additional steps on the upper level that the celebrant and servers mounted to stand at the altar itself. Thus the community looking at Breuer's floor plan in 1956 was used to an altar raised eight steps above the main floor of the church. No wonder some thought Breuer's three steps skimpy.

What about the communion rail? John cited the opinion of Father Schnitzler, a German rubricist who said the rail wasn't required. Could we get along with communion tables at the edge of the sanctuary? In the mid-50s communion tables sounded radical enough to satisfy liturgical innovators like Michael Marx—communicants would stand, not kneel, to receive the host on the tongue—but not so radical as to risk disapproval by the bishop.

How close to the people should the altar be? Father Paschal Botz—dogmatic theology prof, co-editor of the pioneering *Short Breviary* in English, master of dry wit and fishing the Watab—thought it ought to be near the throne lest the choir rather than the altar become the main element in the sanctuary. Godfrey took the opposite view, closer to the people is better, "togetherness" counterbalances "otherness." He quoted the pope. In the final plan the precise location of the altar was decided on a hint from Joachim in a letter to Breuer in December 1953 that sliding the altar slightly forward on the north-south axis of the church would achieve the golden section, a classic linear ratio prized by geometers and artists.

We did not know what the altar would look like. My notes say that someone suggested that it might be "transparent." What that meant I don't remember. Paschal said that the richness of the altar furnishings was important. Cloud did not favor a baldachin, the ceremonial roof over the altar, raised on posts or columns like the one in the old church. On the contrary, John said, posts convey a sense of stability. Cloud thought a canopy concentrating light on the altar would lend sufficient emphasis. Godfrey concurred. Others asked whether we wanted that sort of theatrical effect. Would the apse mural heighten the sacred character of the altar? someone asked. The architect's loose sketch of monumental figures on the screen led us to think so.

The possibility of a prelate celebrating Mass *versus populum* occasioned another set of concerns. It's a key to the mentality we were coming from that the prospect of just any priest celebrating Mass facing the people wasn't in the picture. Even though the altar was freestanding, we all assumed that the ordinary celebrant would have his back to the congregation. When we got around to planning the downstairs chapels for the Brothers and the parish, we initially placed the altars in both chapels close to the wall and only later moved the altars forward so that priests could stand at them facing the people.

How to reserve the Blessed Sacrament was a question. We were used to a tall cylindrical tabernacle covered with a veil in the liturgical color of the day, but that style wouldn't work on a freestanding altar. Should we consider a separate Blessed Sacrament chapel? We didn't give that option serious thought. We were accustomed to reciting the Divine Office—the Liturgy of the Hours—in the presence of the Blessed Sacrament, and we assumed we would continue to do so in the new church. Possibly the altar could be designed to accommodate a low, wide tabernacle centered so as to be accessible from either side. Putting the tabernacle there and deciding where to place altar cards, candles, and the missal stand would require further thought once the dimensions of the altar were known.

Where to Seat the Brothers

A touchy issue that we were to come back to repeatedly
in the coming year was where to seat the Brothers when they
joined the rest of the community for Mass or ceremonies in
the upper church. Breuer's original plan showed a horseshoe-
shaped monastic choir hinged on the abbot's throne and focused on the altar. We were still vague about the number of
choir stalls we wanted, but it would surely be well over a hundred. Could the number of stalls be increased to include the
Brothers? That was what Colman recommended rather than
separate seating. Benedict agreed with him: a single choir for
everybody.

Well, but wouldn't that mean a noticeable gap in the choir
when the Brothers weren't there, which was most of the time?
On ordinary days they had their own Divine Office in English
downstairs at the same time as the Fathers and Clerics had
theirs in Latin upstairs, and on weekday mornings they had an
early Mass so some could be free to serve private Masses when
the first shift of priests came down.

Aside from the objection to a gap of thirty or forty empty
seats in the choir, there was the canonical consideration that
the Brothers were not members of the clergy and therefore
shouldn't be seated in the sanctuary. Whether this was a valid
point was debated. John, our canonist, thought it could be argued either way. True, the Brothers were not clerics, but on the
other hand they were monks. He cited practice at the German
monasteries of Münsterschwarzach and Maria Laach, where
the entire monastic community sat in the choir. Someone suggested adopting the practice of Saint Meinrad Abbey and putting the Brothers in the back row, where empty seating would
not be conspicuous. The only point on which all agreed was
that wherever the Brothers were located, they ought to be able
to see both the altar and the throne. That's where we left it for
the moment.

Approaching the choir down the east window aisle.

December 18–20, 1956

IV Marcel Breuer and Hamilton Smith joined us on December 18. It was Ham's first visit. He had recently joined the firm on the recommendation of Eero Saarinen, with whom he had done his first work. He was in his early thirties. He was to become as familiar a figure as Breuer, in some respects Breuer's alter ego during the church project and for years afterwards. Along with Bob Gatje, he played a major role in thinking through the challenges of design and construction of the church and interpreting it in later years. Writing an appreciation in *Saint John's at 150*, he said that Breuer's plan for the church was fully realized, a rare experience for an architect, and he, Ham, considered it Breuer's finest achievement.

Meeting with us on December 18, Breuer prefaced his remarks by explaining that his initial sketch of the church was schematic. It was part of the comprehensive plan for Saint John's in 1953. Since then, he said, he had thought more about the church plan. Here were some of the main refinements. He had introduced a lantern above the altar. He said it was about half the size of the ceiling of the room we were meeting in, the Alumni Lounge. He did not say that someone at Saint John's had suggested the lantern, but I seem to recall that Cloud and others had thought that opening the roof to mark the centrality of the altar would be a good idea, even if structurally tricky.

Another major advance on the schematic drawings was Breuer's refinement of the trapezoidal form of the structure. Instead of the rigidly straight line of the side walls in the initial sketch, Breuer now introduced a slight curve which mysteriously turned the geometrical shape into an organic form. Indoors the sight line down the side aisles bowed just enough to recede into infinity. Some regarded this nuance as perhaps the finest effect in the design of the church.

Among other modifications of Breuer's first sketch, the ceiling was now to be left unpainted. Gold leaf would be limited to the ceiling in the lantern. The choir would be enclosed with a masonry wall. A crypt under the chapter house might provide a site for the Saint Peregrin shrine or for private altars. Someone asked whether the main altar of the old church might be preserved somewhere in the new church as the altar of Saint Peregrin. On a more serious note, Godfrey questioned how well antiphonal recitation of the psalms would work in the U-shaped choir. At the wide end of the choir the two sides would be farther apart than was customary in even the largest of the historic monastic churches. Breuer said that he thought bringing the two sides close together at the abbot's throne would compensate for the unusual spread at the other end.

Our collective impulse to decorate things showed up repeatedly. Could the cross on the banner be colored, perhaps gold? Could the cross be Benedictine or Greek rather than Latin? Could there be a statue on the banner? Breuer thought that graphic elements—Saint Benedict, Saint John the Baptist—might better be developed at the doorway, a suggestion that was to result in Doris Caesar's gaunt bronze statue of John gesturing toward the baptismal font in the finished atrium. Could the banner be given an overall mosaic treatment? This was conceivable given the right artist, responded Breuer, the diplomat. As we got to know him we were to observe more than once how deft he was at listening soberly to any proposal, however far out or downright silly, while hewing to his basic aesthetic of honest materials skillfully handled for a simple effect.

Aside from our decorative instincts we also asked questions about structure and construction. We were curious about the exterior finish of the church. Would it be white concrete? The answer was that no, a concrete exterior would not be feasible in this climate. The plan called for insulation between the concrete structure and a granite facing. The granite would not be variegated; color would be selected after looking at local options;

joints would be flush to convey the impression of a continuous
sheath of stone.

What about the banner itself? Never mind decorating it.
Was it a Christian symbol or a commercial symbol? Breuer
thought that the banner with its presentation of the cross and
the bells would not look commercial. "I really don't believe that
if the banner is built anyone will find the faintest comparison
with commercialism." For that matter, he said, neither was the
tower an inherently Christian symbol. Ham Smith chimed in
to say that the banner was a sympathetic form for the façade of
the proposed church. Breuer added that architects had experimented with the tower as a modern form without too much suc-
cess, and that with this church a tower would look too thin and
fragile. We left it at that except that Lancelot reported a concern
among his parishioners that the banner might not be stable in
a high wind, or at least that the exposed bells might ring in a
high wind. Breuer replied, "If it is such a wind, perhaps the bells
should ring."

Breuer and Smith stayed until the afternoon of the 20th.
An indication of the exploratory nature of our discussion is the
range of other topics broached.

One was where to put a parish office. We thought maybe off
the cloister walk at one of the side entrances to the church. That
is what we finally settled on at the east entrance, only to discover
once the church was in use that the space was cramped and not
suitably located for any sort of confidential business. It was to
be 1983 before the parish built its own center out on Fruit Farm
Road. Meanwhile pastors used the room at the east entrance to the
church as an easily accessible chapel for the parishioners, several of
them elderly, who came to daily Mass. In 2009 it would be opened
into the main body of the church and restructured as a Blessed
Sacrament chapel.

We talked about providing the Preps with the shortest route
from their quarters in the Quad to daily Mass in the lower
chapel by adding a stairway just inside the west entrance of the

church to match the one planned at the east entrance. I don't recall that we gave this serious thought, possibly because there was tacit understanding that the days of the Preps in the Quad were numbered; two years after the church was dedicated they moved to the new Prep School on Observatory Hill.

A third question was whether to extend the organ gallery around the interior perimeter of the church to form a balcony for private prayer removed from traffic on the main floor but still focused on the Blessed Sacrament on the main altar. Oddly enough, Breuer thought or at least said that this would be feasible and possibly pleasing. Smith didn't think so and pointed out that there were plenty of medium-scale spaces already introduced into the volume of the church.

Heating got cursory attention with a glance at locating equipment in a basement under the chapter house.

Breuer made an observation about lighting that at least partially explains why many people have found the church lighting unsatisfactory. He said that you want fully lighted areas and areas of shade in such a large space. You don't want the uniform illumination of a supermarket. It is possible that the lighting engineers achieved more shade than he had in mind.

An Alternate Design

The most unexpected exchange of the whole meeting took place on Wednesday evening at nine in the art library when Abbot Baldwin asked almost casually whether Breuer could sketch out an alternate design! What prompted this query I don't know. It may have reflected the unease of some members of the community with the Breuer design.

Whatever the abbot was thinking when he posed the question, Breuer responded with something close to emotion. To produce another design, he said, would take time and the same intensity he put into this one. The end result would probably be worse confusion. In choosing a building one does not have the luxury of selecting one of several existing things, he said. In architecture you buy something that doesn't yet exist. In short, one doesn't just create two different, equally worthy plans. Contact with the client, working with him during design is most important and more valuable than commissioning several alternate plans.

This eloquent response marked a critical stage in planning the church, even though it wasn't published and no one present commented on its significance as a silent turning point in our own thinking. We were not simply looking at some sketches that an architect had come up with on an afternoon in the office. What we were looking at in the schematic drawings had required the time and concentrated thought of a master architect. By contracting him for working drawings we had signified approval of his conception of a church that would meet our needs. Without anyone saying it, we would proceed to refine the plan and decide a wealth of practical details with a new seriousness.

Private Chapels

Meeting the next morning, we talked about chapels for the celebration of private Masses.

In the pre–Vatican II church priests were expected to celebrate Mass daily, with or without a congregation. At Saint John's, with its dozens of professors and staff members who were priests, this meant lots of altars somewhere in the church to accommodate three half-hour pre-breakfast shifts of men coming to a common sacristy to prepare to say private Masses. Pre-breakfast because the Mass could only be offered and Communion received by those fasting from food and drink since midnight. Each priest was accompanied to an altar by a server carrying cruets of water and wine—Brothers on the first shift, other monks or students on the second and third shifts—and the students needed a separate place to leave their jackets or coats and don a surplice.

The thirty-four now mostly unused elegant little side chapels in the basement of the church give silent witness to a Eucharistic

discipline customary throughout the Church prior to Vatican
II. The question before us in December 1956 was not whether
this discipline would continue but how to provide for it in the
new church. How many private altars were really needed? How
thoroughly should they be separated from one another? That
there should be only one altar in the upstairs church had been
understood from the beginning. If the liturgical revival meant
anything it meant that the Eucharist was the sacrament of community, of the faithful gathered around a single altar, not scattered semi-privately among many. Ironically the new church at
Collegeville, a renowned liturgical center, would straddle two
worlds, upstairs boldly accommodating the Christian community, downstairs still providing the setting for a long established
individual piety.

Before he went back to New York, Marcel Breuer advised us
that floor plan and seating capacity were two fundamentals we
needed to settle before he could do more work.

I might remark in passing that seeing how ideas and sketches
led to exact specifications for parts of the Breuer church taught
me not to take so much as a doorknob for granted. It perhaps
bears emphasis that in the end virtually every detail in the finished church was to be Breuer's. Ham Smith was to observe on a
later visit that he had not known Mr. Breuer to give his time so
fully to any other project.

January–March 1957

V Three months were to pass before Ham Smith returned on March 20, 1957. In the interval major elements of the church plan gradually took the shape
they were to have in the finished building. Three persistent questions recurred. One of them was the relation of the altar to the
congregation. Another was whether the side windows should be

clear glass. A third and most vexing one was where to seat the
Brothers in the upper church and how to lay out the space for
them in a Brothers chapel in the lower church. Rather than walk
through these items and a range of others meeting by meeting,
let me try to describe what people said on these and other issues
and how we finally arrived at some answers in a series of meetings from January to March.

The first months of 1957 saw the interior of the church
gradually take shape with actual numbers and dimensions. We
weren't yet into materials and finishes, but by March we had
settled that the body of the church would seat 1,130 people and
the balcony an additional 508. There would be 204 upper choir
stalls in six rows spaced three feet six inches from the back of
one row to the back of the next and twenty-eight inches wide,
an improvement over the twenty-inch seats in the old church
that cramped the style of Father Matthew Kiess and other ample
monks. Later we were to approve widening the stalls by two
inches and reducing the number to 186.

The altar would be five feet wide to allow for a low tabernacle in the center of the altar, accessible from either side, and
nine feet long. The length was a compromise. John, master of
ceremonies, thought that ten feet was as short as we could go
and still accommodate priest, deacon, subdeacon, and MC
without unseemly crowding when they were all at the altar
simultaneously during a solemn high Mass. He pointed out
that we were used to a main altar fourteen feet long. Cloud,
Benedict and Michael thought that five by eight feet would be
a more pleasing proportion, and that as a freestanding form
the altar would allow ministers and servers to wrap around the
corners to avoid jostling one another. In the end the block that
was cut out of white Vermont marble was to be 60-by-93-inches
after further fine-tuning by the architect, but that was two years
in the future.

After mulling over the psychology of the Brothers with
Father Richard Eckroth, their superior, and the canonical

niceties about where to place a group of men who were in monastic vows but not clerical orders, we decided that the eighty lower stalls would do nicely for the Brothers when they attended liturgical functions in the upper church. Since eighty stalls was more than they needed, nobody would have to sit in the back rows where there were a few seats from which you couldn't see the abbot's throne. Everybody would have a clear view of the altar and whatever action might be going on in the sanctuary.

Access from the window aisle also meant that the Brothers could take their place without walking through the sanctuary or disturbing whatever might be going on in choir. The times when the Brothers attended a liturgy in the upper church had generally been limited to the Mass on Sundays and major feasts and the early morning solemn requiem Masses for deceased members of the community on the third, seventh, thirtieth days, and first-year memorials of their death. Richard assured us that the Brothers—well, most of them—were happy to have their status recognized and would welcome this arrangement. None of them were present to speak for themselves.

In the Brothers chapel downstairs there would be seating for 120, arranged in two banks of stalls facing each other for antiphonal recitation of the Divine Office. The other, larger downstairs chapel intended for use by both the parish and the Prep School would seat 480. There were to be thirty-four side chapels for private Masses; Florian wondered whether we really needed that many. How to make room for so many side chapels would require further thought, but we agreed that we didn't want any of them in a crypt under the chapter house.

We had some questions about the throne and the communion tables. The first question about the throne was whether it ought to be a permanent fixture. This was a monastic church, not a cathedral. Wouldn't a throne for the abbot be confused with a bishop's *cathedra*? In the old church the abbot's throne was to one side of the lower level of the sanctuary facing the other side of the choir, not the congregation. It was the abbot's place in choir.

Could the throne in the new church, even though separate from both sides of choir, serve as the abbot's choir stall? Make the throne permanent but provide it with a prie-dieu including a shelf for the abbot's choir books and we would have an abbatial choir stall, not an episcopal throne. Abbot Baldwin was to use it that way during his first years in the new church. The throne was permanent, the prie-dieu removable on occasions when the abbot or a bishop presided at the liturgy. After a few years Baldwin moved into a regular choir stall. Sometime in the '80s—I can't pin down just when—the prie-dieu went into storage and nobody worried about whether the throne was a *cathedra* or not.

Whether the communion tables should be permanent or might be wooden tables to be set out when wanted was another question. Opinion in the committee favored making them permanent, but we didn't really know how to use them. In the pre–Vatican II church there were not usually crowds of people going to Communion, nor was Communion given under both kinds. Catholics were used to coming up to the communion rail, kneeling, putting their hands under the communion cloth conveniently flipped up and over the rail by the altar boys (no girls) before Communion, and opening their mouths to receive the thin circular host on the tongue.

At a communion table there would be no cloth to cover your hands, so what did you do with them? Maybe rest them on the table? If so, how high and how wide should the table be, and should more than one person be able to stand at it at a time? In mid-February we practiced with a mock-up of a communion table, decided that thirty-nine inches would be a good height with the priest behind it on a twelve-inch riser, the table itself 1-by-4-feet. We were still of two minds about whether the communion tables should be fixed or movable and whether we wanted two or four.

Ham Smith's March visit was a particularly important meeting, as interesting for the questions that came up and were left unsettled as it was for agreement on elements of the plan that had been thoroughly studied and would not change significantly in the working drawings. The layout of the sanctuary and choir was essentially settled. There was still some debate about where to put the organ console, but that was because we didn't yet know who would build the organ. Final thinking about the apse mural also awaited a decision about the organ builder, not to mention that we had not yet chosen an artist to do the mural.

Balcony, Window, Banner, Bells

Breuer had reworked the design of the balcony. It was to provide a third of the seating in the body of the church. It would now be cantilevered from four great piers lined up behind the last row of pews in the nave and anchored in massive footings beneath the floor of the crypt. It would echo the slightly angled placement of the pews on the main floor to focus on the altar.

The façade of pre-cast concrete hexagons was new. Ham explained that it was designed to make the wall more solid, to give an impression of greater height, and to provide "almost limitless" possibilities for design within the overall pattern. The first question asked by one of the native Minnesotans on the committee was whether the hexagons wouldn't catch snow in the winter. Several were concerned about heating a wall of glass. None of us could know that two years down the line the limitless possibilities for the design of the stained glass to be put in all those hexagons—all 486 of them—would come down to two competing designs that would polarize the committee and make for some tense moments between the abbot and Breuer himself.

On the entrance plaza the banner had been greatly refined from the primitive schematic drawing. It now took on the

Looking west at floor
level in the back of the
church with balcony
piers and window wall
hexagons on either side.

function of a great parabolic arch over the entrance to the church surmounted by a vertically cantilevered slab rising more than one hundred feet above the plaza, with a horizontal opening to hold the five bells from the towers of the old church and a vertical opening above the bells for a Latin cross.

The bells or rather how to ring them was the subject of some discussion. The architect had consulted the I. T. Verdin Company. They told him the bells could be mechanically struck or swung. Abbot Baldwin asked whether they could be rung manually. Some of us thought that would be good. Ham said swinging them would not cause stress problems. No one foresaw the malfunctioning mechanisms and cracked bells that would limit use of the bells in the new location.

Other items were discussed but not settled. The importance of acoustical separation between the crypt chapels got lots of emphasis and resulted in the highly effective placement of solid concrete walls to create acoustically separate zones for the private Mass chapels, the large chapel for the Prep School and parish, and the smaller Brothers chapel.

How private the private Mass chapels should be was a question. Abbot Baldwin thought a wooden screen cutting off visual contact with the corridor was advisable. How to arrange elements in the parish chapel got some attention. The abbot didn't want it to be called the parish chapel, but as yet it didn't have another name. An unresolved question was whether to reserve the Blessed Sacrament there as well as at the main altar upstairs and in the Brothers chapel. Would we need to get canonical permission to reserve the Blessed Sacrament in all three chapels? If we didn't have reservation in the Brothers chapel how would that affect the Brothers' recitation of the Divine Office, and where would the whole community go for its daily processional visit to the Blessed Sacrament after the noon meal?

March 21–22, 1957

VI After a solemn high Mass for the feast of Saint Benedict on the morning of March 21, we had an open meeting in the afternoon with Mssrs. Gausman and Keller of the Gausman and Moore engineering firm to talk about heating and ventilation. The first topic was radiant heating in the nave. Breuer had told us in December that he favored a split heating system: radiant heating in the body of the church to maintain a steady minimum temperature in cold weather; a forced air system on the perimeter of the space and in the crypt to adjust to outdoor temperature changes from day to day and provide ventilation.

HVAC and All That

Some of the members of the committee were skeptical about radiant heating: would it work, would it last, wouldn't the pipes corrode, wouldn't it leak, what would you do if it did leak, could some fluid other than water be used, and was it economical or adequate or both in Minnesota winters? The engineers assured us that it would work beautifully and that similar systems were in use elsewhere in Minnesota.

To get ahead of our story, the system was installed and functioned as the engineers said it would. The only glitch occurred in the west cloister walk one fall when the water in the pipes froze. Rather than tear up the brick floor to repair the resulting damage, a baseline radiator running the length of the corridor was installed, precisely the sort of visual clutter that Breuer took pains to avoid.

Ham Smith made the architect's point about keeping the look uncluttered as he introduced the topic of heating and ventilation. The idea was to avoid visible duct work and heating appliances. Ventilation would be through registers at the base of the side windows and a grill under the leading edge of the organ gallery, air return through the plenum under the choir stalls and circulating fans in one of the ceiling trusses. The entire crypt would be heated and ventilated by forced air. We would have to wait until we could walk into the completed church to appreciate how neatly mechanical features were incorporated into the structural lines and materials of the space itself.

Would the system be noisy? we asked. Not at all, the engineers replied. All of the equipment except the ceiling fans would be buried under the baptistery, acoustically isolated behind concrete walls. The circulating and exhaust fans in the ceiling trusses would be virtually silent. The whole presentation was reassuring but not entirely accurate. In the completed church acoustical isolation of the mechanical room was excellent, but from the start the ceiling fans needed to be turned off during liturgical services because they were so audible. We also imagined, I guess, that the church would be cooler in the summer than the old church, which it probably is marginally. At any rate, no one breathed a word about air conditioning, a concession to comfort in church that was hardly Catholic and certainly not monastic.

Religious Art

I haven't said anything about devotional art, but that is not because the subject didn't come up during Ham's visit. Were there to be no shrines of any sort associated with the main altar? In the old church there were marble side altars, one dedicated to the Sacred Heart, the other to the Blessed Virgin. There was also a much visited shrine of Mary at the back of the church in a good-sized, well-lighted space at the base of the north tower. If side altars were not appropriate in the sanctuary, could devotional use be made of the space behind the choir, maybe a shrine in each corner? And what about stained glass in the side windows? Did we want clear glass windows in a church? This question would continue to rankle some members of the committee for another three years.

There would, of course, be stained glass in the hexagons of the north wall, although no design had yet been considered, but wouldn't John the Baptist in stained glass be fitting for the center door at the entrance to the atrium, or a figure of Christ on a center post in the doorway leading from the atrium into the church? We talked briefly about Stations of the Cross but reached no conclusion except that we would want stations in the parish chapel as well as in the main body of the church. The polychrome plaster stations in the old church would not fit Breuer's church, but contemporary work might complement the stark white walls Breuer planned.

Ham Smith went back to New York on March 22 with many features of the plan reviewed and ready for working drawings. There hadn't yet been much discussion of materials other than concrete and concrete block. The nave was to be paved with quarry tile rather than brick, Ham told us. This decision would be reversed at a later stage in planning. Would a different paving be preferable in the sanctuary and the choir stalls, he asked: perhaps terrazzo or wood, or as Lancelot suggested, rubber tile, which would be easier to clean than wood? We assumed that the interior walls would be painted white upstairs and down. Nothing was said about the finish of stalls, pews, and other furnishings.

May 3–4, 1957

VII

What we talked about when Ham returned with Breuer on May 3–4 were the organ, a critical report on ringing the bells, and again and finally radiant heating in the atrium, nave, and cloister walks.

Organ

That the new church called for a new organ was not questioned. The old church had two organs, one of them—the original church organ modified over the years—in the gallery over the entrance, the other in a chamber behind the north side of the choir. Neither would be adequate in the much larger new church.

In April 1957 Father Gerard Farrell was abbey organist and Father Bartholomew Sayles schola director. Members of the church planning committee met with them in April and again during Breuer's visit in May. Gerard put it simply and comprehensively when he said that we needed an organ to accompany the monastic choir and the congregation and for solo work. He was not sure that Walter Holtkamp, though eminent, was best suited to build an organ for liturgical use. He thought Ernest White, also eminent, ought to be considered, since he had done the organ at Saint Benedict's Abbey in Atchison, Kansas. At least we ought to shop around a bit and not simply go with Holtkamp because Breuer liked him. Whether or not White ought to be involved was an argument Gerard had mostly with himself since none of the rest of us knew much about contemporary organ builders. In the end we were to agree on Holtkamp after the musicians and liturgists gave some thought to Casavant as well as White.

Where to put the organ was a question we could all discuss. Nobody was enthusiastic about locating it behind the apse screen. We thought it would be overpowering in choir and even then perhaps not fill the church. High in the balcony against the window wall would be acoustically splendid but would probably require a second, smaller organ closer in to accompany the choir. Breuer had looked at hanging it on a side wall like the organs introduced into some great medieval churches but concluded this was not feasible. Behind the apse screen looked like the only option.

The builder would need to tell us how many of the interstices in the screen must be left open. Holtkamp had said at least two-thirds, Breuer thought three-fourths to be safe. He discreetly urged us to get on with commissioning an artist to do the apse

mural by mentioning that he thought Jean Charlot, whom he
knew, would be a good choice. He also noted that he had decided against piercing the wall behind the organ with a pattern
of small apertures to admit light.

Where to place the organ console was debated. There was no
question of a grand organ case. One of the things Breuer liked
about Holtkamp was their agreement that the organ should
be heard but not seen. This meant that we were talking about
a modest console designed not to attract attention. I think we
had tacitly assumed that the organist would be seated somewhere in the choir, as was the case in the old church. However,
Gerard now suggested that the console be located down front
in a recessed area on the east edge of the sanctuary between the
lower stalls and the altar. Abbot Baldwin's first reaction was that
this would be too conspicuous; Breuer assured him that the area
could be deep enough so the console and the organist would not
interrupt anybody's line of sight. We adopted this solution, but
in the working drawings Breuer moved the console to the other
side of the sanctuary to make room for a reading desk or ambo
to the right of the altar.

Aside from understanding that the organ would need to
be good-sized to fill the volume of the church, we did not talk
about specifications. This was to be handled by Gerard and the
other organists working with Holtkamp. We agreed that small
organs would be wanted in both of the chapels downstairs
and considered possible locations. In the parish chapel a crying room for parents with infants was tentatively planned to
be centered in the back between the stairways coming down
from the atrium. That's where Bartholomew thought the organ
should go. Lancelot, the pastor, preferred the organ closer to
the altar, where the organist could see and be seen for congre-
gational singing.

Where to put the Peregrin shrine came into the discussion too. Since the 1920s Saint John's had been in possession of
some skeletal remains purporting to be the relic of a Roman

adolescent martyred in the third century. Masked in bejeweled gauze in a glass casket behind an ornamental grill under the main altar in the lower chapel, Peregrin—a symbolic name meaning "traveler"—was always an object of curiosity if not piety for new students and visitors to the campus. Where should this object of piety be placed when the old church was vacated? Minority opinion favored decent burial next to the abbots in the cemetery. Failing outright burial, discreet disposition of the martyr's remains somewhere in the crypt of the new church looked like the next best thing. We left it up to Breuer to decide where to put this relic but barred using the altar in the parish chapel as a display case.

Bells

On May 3 Breuer also reported his consultation with I. T. Verdin on how to sound the bells once they were mounted on the bell platform of the banner. There were five bells in the twin towers, and clock faces on all four sides of both towers. Bells 3 and 2 struck the quarter hours, bell 1 the hours. For Sunday Mass and other occasions, the Novices rang the bells manually from chambers in the bell towers, two bells in the north tower, three in the south. Ringing the big one took two Novices, one riding up while the other came down on opposite ends of a rope that ran in a great loop over the wheel above.

According to Breuer, Verdin said that bells in the exposed location proposed by the architect could be struck mechanically and rung either mechanically or manually but not both. However, the firm wanted nothing to do with swinging the bells in that location lest they fall. Breuer took the bellmakers' concern with a grain of salt, since they had an interest in installing a system of electrically struck hammers in the bells. However, he would consult another bell maker on the risk of the bells falling. We went on to talk about possibly ringing the bells manually with ropes let down through the roof of the atrium or outside of it. Whether we wanted the bells to strike

the hours was another question raised but not answered in
this meeting.

As a kind of postscript, I might note that before the banner
was built, there was probably no one on the committee who
realized just how heavy and well anchored it would be. The
committee did not deal with tonnages of concrete and steel.
When the time came in late fall 1959 to pour the footings and
the massive tie rods between them some twenty feet beneath the
entry plaza, we were impressed with the number of heavy steel
rods buried in the concrete. The same ratio of steel to concrete
continued in the structure of the legs and arch. The vertical
slab constituting the banner itself was a closely woven network
of steel rods encased in precise formwork to receive successive
pourings of concrete. About 2,500 tons of concrete and steel
went into making the banner. Breuer had good reason to think
that it wouldn't wobble when the bells were rung.

We had another round of questions and doubts about radiant heating in the floor of the nave, atrium, and cloister walks.
No new issues surfaced. Abbot Baldwin finally called for a vote
on radiant heating by the seven committee members present
and got five affirmatives, two abstentions. This was taken as approval of the architect's split heating plan, but notes from subse-
quent meetings record lingering doubts about the advisability of
relying on radiant heating for such a large area as the main floor
of the church.

A wealth of other items, some of them concerning quite
small details like the proper incline for book rests in the choir
stalls and where to locate holy water stoups, crowded into this
highly interesting meeting. Some major items got a first hearing.
We noted that church lighting, especially choir lighting, was a
major element that we would need to deal with in due course.
Breuer described the size and finish of the granite slabs that he
had in mind as facing for the exterior of the church. He referred
to cabinet work in the private Mass chapels. All in all we seemed
to be making good progress.

VIII

Summer 1957 marked the high point of attention to working drawings in Breuer's New York office. By contrast, there was a lull in the planning committee's work. Many of the decisions affecting how the interior of the church would look had been made. A new Roman decree obliged us to look again at where to reserve the Blessed Sacrament. The ruling seemed to prohibit placing the tabernacle on an altar where Mass was said facing the people. Putting it on an altar facing the wall or *versus chorum* was permitted.

In a community meeting called in October to consider the impact of the decree, John, in his double role as canonist and liturgist, gave it as his opinion that for purposes of compliance with the Roman ruling, we could consider the altar permanently oriented *versus chorum* and therefore a permissible site for the tabernacle. The Blessed Sacrament could be moved to another altar on the presumably rare occasions when the Eucharist was to be celebrated *versus populum*. Just to be safe he suggested checking this bit of casuistry with Saint John's Father Ulric Beste, a noted canonist who taught at Sant' Anselmo in Rome, and whose hefty *Introductio in Codicem* was authoritative and widely used in seminaries. We left it at that, went ahead with designing a low tabernacle for the altar, and reserved the Blessed Sacrament there until liturgical reforms after Vatican II ruled out keeping the Blessed Sacrament on the main altar, period.

Cold Spring Granite

A major item that would radically affect how the church looked came up in July when Breuer informed us that Cold Spring Granite's price for the granite facing was considerably higher than expected. It looked like $3 a square foot on the side walls of the church, $2 on the chapter house. This brought the architect's estimate of the cost of granite to $140,000. This price tag did not include granite paving in the entrance plaza, the balcony, and the Blessed Virgin shrine. Did we want to sheathe the church in local granite regardless of the cost?

The committee took a Stearns County approach to this question. Lancelot said that maybe John Alexander, owner of the company, quoted a deliberately high price to the architect because it would become public but expected to give Saint John's a better deal. Abbot Baldwin added that the charge for the rough granite blocks laid up on the exterior of the new monastic wing five years earlier—$30,000—was quite low. Godfrey cited a difference of at least $80,000 between something and something—my notes don't indicate what. A procedure was proposed: tell Breuer that we want the granite, but tell Alexander we can't afford it.

This solution was not universally favored. Some members thought we should tell Breuer to look for another material. John, with his usual discretion, counseled holding off on our response to Breuer over the weekend—this was on Friday—and contacting Alexander to say that Breuer needed an immediate answer but we were hesitating because of the cost. Everybody thought this was worth trying.

At a meeting after supper on Monday evening we learned the results. The abbot and John Alexander had had a conversation on Saturday. Baldwin was cagey about how the conversation came about; he said John Alexander "sneaked up" on him when he was alone. The upshot of their conversation was that John and Florian called on Alexander on Monday and came home with a letter from him saying he would give us the granite at direct cost for labor and materials, then knock off 33 percent as his donation. We still didn't have a precise estimate on the cost—Alexander maintained that Breuer had not yet given Cold Spring the complete plans—but it looked as if we could have granite facing for around $100,000 rather than $150,000. The committee agreed with Lancelot that this was not a bad deal, and Breuer was told to go ahead with the granite. In due course stonemasons from Cold Spring Granite would lay the stone as Alexander suggested.

The blueprints came in October and the project was put out for bids. McGough Construction Company of Saint Paul was one of the contractors who got a set of the plans on October 10, although Jim McGough was reported to be cool to the plan and not fond of exposed concrete. Colman said Charles McGough was eager for the job. November 8 was set for opening the general contractors' bids. Mechanical and electrical bids were due on November 6. Ray Hermanson, who continued to function as a consultant to the committee, held out the hope that construction might yet begin in late fall.

Sound System and Lighting

In a series of meetings during October the committee continued to mull over such items as brick flooring for the sanctuary, floodlighting, lighting in general, the power demands of church lighting, heating, and ventilation. Abbot Baldwin thought floodlighting was an extravagance; Hermanson noted that it was not an item of significant expense. Should the lights—some of the lights, all of the lights—be on dimmers? Would this save money? Could the Rambusch firm do the lighting? The architect estimated $25,000 for lighting, and this could be subcontracted. Placement of holy water stoups, the dozen consecration crosses and candleholders on the sidewalls, the granite panels in the main doorway to the nave all came in for attention.

We had another go at the clear-glass side windows. Glazing for the windows was included in the contract now out for bids, but this could be changed without altering the dimensions of the opening. A stronger frame would be needed for stained glass. The contract called for single glazed moving sections which could be opened for ventilation. Screens could be added but were not included in the contract. For thirty-three years there were to be no screens despite birds, chipmunks, and other crea-

tures of the wild that came in through the open windows. Abbot
Timothy Kelly finally said enough was enough and ordered
screens put on the windows when swarms of mosquitoes spoiled
a heavily attended event in the church on a sticky summer night
in the '90s.

A special meeting on October 24 considered the electrical contract. Fathers Fintan Bromenshenkel and Casper Keogh
joined us along with Mr. Joe Roske, chief engineer at the powerhouse. Mr. Moore of Gausman and Moore broke the news to us
that peak load for the church would be 250 kilowatt hours, an
impressive figure even for the non-technicians among us when
we were told that heretofore 375 kW was peak load for the whole
campus. There were thirty-five motors in the building, six on the
bells alone. Moore estimated that floodlighting alone could account for 35 kW.

He did not strongly back the specifications for floodlighting. He thought they were designed for New York. He was also
not much in favor of dimmers, although he granted that dimmers could result in a saving on light bulbs. He thought that the
architect's dimmers were not meant to extend the life of light
bulbs but to create atmosphere, as was done in some Protestant
churches. The electrical contractor could provide adequate reading light without using dimmers.

On a related topic, it should be noted in fairness to Gausman and Moore that they had nothing to do with the sound
system beyond providing circuits. Moore told us the sound
system would be installed under a separate contract. When the
system came, it was limited to directional speakers tastefully
concealed in the baldachin. They proved to be totally under-
sized for the volume of the church. Once the church was in use,
we put standing loudspeakers in the side aisles for big crowds
and then after a few years hung a humungous cluster of speakers above the baldachin. Irreverent younger monks dubbed it
Zardoz after the fake deity in the movie of the same name. It
hovered over the altar until 1997 without providing much gain

in audibility, although its prominence made you think you could hear better.

Bids were opened on November 8 and were higher than expected. McGough's was the lowest, but it did not include a whole range of items needed to complete the church. Of these, the granite facing and the north wall glass were the largest items, but choir stalls and pews, altars and cabinet work also had to be provided, not to mention roads, parking, and landscaping. McGough was eager to do the job and eager to get going. They estimated four hundred working days for construction and were ready to start in two or three weeks.

Cost Estimate

The church committee met with the Senior Council on November 11 to take a realistic look at the probable cost of the completed church. McGough's bid was $1,663,000. Adding granite ($130,000), glass in the north wall ($30,000 plus installation), pews and choir stalls ($65,000), altars and cabinet work made it look as if something more than $2 million would be needed to construct the completed church. Moreover, McGough was now suggesting a cost-plus contract out of concern that their bid was too low. Abbot Baldwin suggested a ceiling of $2 million for construction, with the possibility of leaving the church only partially furnished. No one thought the Chapter was likely to buy this approach.

How to reduce the cost was the topic of conversation with Marcel Breuer and Ham Smith that evening. The combination of ways we thought of to cut costs was standard. Could we economize on lighting? How about those dimmers and those floodlights? Smith cited figures to show that at most a few thousand dollars might be pared off the total construction cost by cutting back on lighting. Breuer made the point that lighting engineers were prone to overlighting and that variations in the density of lighting were what made a space seem brightly lighted. Hence from his point of view the utility of dimmers.

If cutting back on lighting wouldn't save much money, could we get along without the balcony for the time being? What Breuer must have thought of this wistful query I can only guess. He treated it as a serious question and patiently explained that adding the balcony later would be extremely expensive and messy. He might have added that it was needed to achieve the seating capacity we said we needed.

We cast about for other major savings. How about all of that wooden formwork? Lumber alone was running over $100,000. Could the church be constructed in prefabricated sections? What would Nervi think of doing it that way? Breuer responded that he had discussed the structure thoroughly with Nervi and engineers in New York and that building it in prefab sections was totally unfeasible, the weight much too heavy, the span too great.

Then how about leaving the crypt unfinished? Breuer said this was a standard cost-cutting measure: leave the basement unfinished. Before construction was complete the decision would be reversed and the crypt finished at greater expense. Someone finally asked the most obvious question: could we omit the banner for the present? Yes, Breuer said, that would of course be possible. Adding it later would undoubtedly be more difficult and more expensive. Merely trimming back on the plaza and the steps—the prospect of an expanse of steps one hundred feet long had upset some members of the community almost as much as the prospect of clear glass in the side windows—would not save much money.

Thus at the end of the day no significant economies appeared other than some unspecified savings on granite that Smith said were in sight. Breuer expressed himself satisfied with McGough as contractor. He was impressed with their solution of a problem in regard to scaffolding. By contrast, "I cannot believe that they did not notice that the main floor acts as a tie," he said, but added that they knew every other note in the plans. "I think they are quite capable fellows." He mentioned that a supervisor from his office would be on hand during construction, "a whiz at geometry, which is not easy in the church." With that the meeting ended and Breuer went back to New York.

November Chapter Vote

The Chapter met four days later and by a large margin voted not to proceed with construction of the church. Even without the chapter house—removed from the proposal in the course of discussion to make the bid a little more palatable—the figure before the Chapter exceeded $2 million, $2,007,972 to be exact, and this did not include furnishings.

In his capacity as treasurer of the corporation Florian Muggli, never a fan of the Breuer church, reported that this sum added to costs for the new student dormitory and an addition to the powerhouse would bring our indebtedness to well over $4 million. He recommended delaying action for a couple of years. Father Cyril Ortman, pastor of Saint Martin's Parish, was one of the outside Fathers living within a hundred-mile radius of the monastery whom the abbot was obliged to invite to a chapter meeting dealing with an expenditure of more than $30,000. He suggested delaying three years. Father Theodore Krebsbach, pastor of Saint Bernard's Parish in Saint Paul and former dean of the Prep School, seconded the motion. Florian, sensing the mood of the meeting, said that on second thought it seemed better to him not to set a limit.

Thus when the matter finally came to a vote, the question was not whether the community approved the Breuer design, but whether construction ought to be postponed indefinitely. This was the positive spin Abbot Baldwin put on the vote in a letter to Marcel Breuer the next day: "The majority voted that it would be more prudent, from a financial point of view, to postpone construction." The letter had a curiously personal tone. The abbot had sent a telegram the night before and he started by saying, "I think you know how sincerely I regretted having . . . to inform you" of the Chapter's action. He added, "I believe the majority are still very much in favor of doing whatever is possible in order that construction might begin without too great a delay."

Breuer responded as soon as he got the letter, November 19, on an equally personal note: "I have the warmest appreciation of your good words, still more so because I know how you yourself must have been affected by the negative vote of the chapter." He offered to help with fund-raising. He observed that there were only a few changes to be made in the drawings to reflect his most recent thinking. He pointed ahead to the next stage of church planning: the cross, the altars, the artwork, "and other remaining problems" which his office would continue to study.

In a letter dated the next day, Ham Smith itemized changes resulting from their recent visit to Collegeville. Some exterior lighting was removed; the glazing of the side windows remained unspecified; there were slight adjustments in the placement of holy water stoups, lavabos, consecration crosses—fine points indeed. In a final paragraph Smith suggested that the building committee review the need for additional electrical power service, since this could require a transformer vault in the church.

April 1958

IX The committee did not meet again in 1957 or in the early months of 1958. Planning came to a virtual standstill over the winter months as the abbot and the architect joined forces with the business office and the fledgling development staff—basically Father Walter Reger and Isabelle Durenberger—to address the finances of the project.

Florian was at the heart of this discussion; other members of the building committee were not involved, and I have no inside information on what transpired between the chapter meeting on November 15, 1957, which turned down construction of the church and the chapter meeting five months later on April 22, 1958, which approved it with a resounding vote of 103 to 17.

The figure before the Chapter in April was $1,942,859 for the church and the chapter house, $258,555 lower than the sum for the same facilities in November. In his letter of April 15 announcing the chapter meeting the abbot explained that McGough had pared their bid, fund-raising had resulted in gifts and pledges of $250,000, the price of steel and cement had dropped since November, and bids on the new dorm were considerably lower than expected.

One of the keys to the lower bid was cutting $100,000 from construction cost by an inventive approach to supporting formwork for the roof slab that Breuer labeled ingenious and his engineers fully approved.

At the close of this historic chapter meeting some of us young members of the Chapter suggested ringing the bells. The abbot approved. It was a mild April afternoon, a Tuesday two weeks into the Easter season, and the peal rang out over the greening campus, the barnyard empty of cattle for two years now, the newly plowed fields of the Eichs and the Zwillings across the Watab, and the dozen families—Roskes and Rassiers and Kleins and Durenbergers among them—who made up the population of Flynntown. The student population of roughly 100 seminarians, 1,100 college students, and 250 preps wondered what "the Fathers" were celebrating.

Summer of 1958

Saint John's was a thriving community in 1958. Approval of the church meant that two Breuer buildings would be under construction by midsummer, the four-hundred-student college dorm named Thomas Aquinas Hall as well as the church. In June the abbot appointed the dean of the college, Father Arno Gustin—incidentally his classmate—as the new president of Saint John's University, a historic move that separated the offices of abbot and president linked by Alexius Edelbrock in 1875.

It was a boom year for monastic vocations: thirteen Novices were invested on July 10, and seventeen young monks made simple or solemn vows on the Solemnity of Saint Benedict the next day. The whole community numbered 367, many of them in the five priories scattered from Nassau to Tokyo, or in parishes, chaplaincies, and missions closer to home. Not to be overlooked among the notable events of 1958, it was the year Zinsmaster Baking Company put Saint John's Bread on the market, thanks to Walter Reger's efforts.

Fund-raising yielded $304,722.49 for church construction by July. To clear the ground for the church construction site, traffic was diverted to a route cut through the woods behind the water tower and the football field which was to become permanent as a perimeter road to athletic facilities and the Prep School. Ground was broken on May 19. Junior monks, sometimes twelve or fifteen on a single day, provided unskilled labor on the construction site during the summer months.

By early fall great square footings marked off the footprint of the church in a broad excavation from which the fill was dumped into the Watab below the powerhouse to create a causeway to the picnic grounds. By Thanksgiving the gray granite cornerstone of the new church was in place, a solid cube lowered by a crane on a blustery early winter day.

It was an exciting time. We didn't know that by the time the church was dedicated three years later Pope John XXIII would have opened the windows of the Church to a fresh coming of the Spirit. In the heady decade to come, gusts of change would sweep away the devotional climate familiar to generations of monks and make the Breuer design, with its spare and unadorned surfaces, both expressive of the new age and at the same time in some ways outdated.

Within ten years praying the Divine Office and celebrating the Eucharist in Latin would be a thing of the past, and along with it the canonical category of "lay" brothers and sisters. With the whole community at prayer in English, the need for a separate Brothers chapel would disappear. Neither could we know, although we might have guessed, that college students would soon make up their own mind about going to Mass, and that in a few years the structure made larger to accommodate a growing student body would be crowded with students only at Commencement.

Summer 1958

X As construction got under way following chapter approval, we moved ahead into part two of church planning, what Breuer referred to as the cross, the altars, the artwork, "and other remaining problems." After a five-month break the church building committee met on May 6, 1958, with a new charge. Abbot Baldwin introduced the topic. With working drawings complete and construction about to begin, the next concern of the committee needed to be what the abbot called "a set of ideas for art and furnishings." He asked whether we would now be well advised to employ someone as an artistic intermediary between the committee and Breuer.

Art Consultant

Members of the committee chimed in on cue. Godfrey said that he agreed 100 percent on the need for an *artist*— Godfrey underlined words as he spoke—on the need for an *artist* to pass final judgment on art. Michael Marx confessed that he lacked artistic judgment and ventured that we needed an art consultant. But *not* one tied to a church goods house, Godfrey warned. Right, said Michael; we needed an independent art coordinator who could provide Breuer with guidance in sacred art.

Implying artistic deficiencies in the architect prompted Joachim to counter this criticism by saying that he would give

Breuer a free hand in designing furniture and altars. Cloud demurred; Breuer was steeped in materialist functionalism. This sounded pretty bad, but the committee was not well positioned to argue the point since we had all tacitly bought into Michael's plea of artistic incompetence. This was the minor premise of the logic for getting an art consultant: somebody needs to give Breuer artistic guidance; we're not capable; ergo. Our collective diplomatic skill would be tested in the coming months when disagreement about the largest artistic element in the church, the north window, could no longer be avoided. For now, however, it was easy enough for Alfred to defuse any tension by asking for a point of clarification about our contract with Breuer: were the furnishings part of the contract or not? Florian thought not but he would check.

This diversion was all that Abbot Baldwin needed to get back to the only real business of this meeting: Whom shall we get as an art consultant? Cloud said we should get a good coordinator. Godfrey named Cloud, who promptly declined. Lancelot thought we might ask Barry Byrnes' advice. Colman opined that we needed a little more warmth and Catholicism than Breuer could give us. Michael, feigning sudden illumination, asked whether Frank Kacmarcik might do.

My notes tell me that at that point I inquired about the committee's continued role, possibly through a subcommittee on art. Alfred thought a subcommittee was a good idea, but the idea died there, probably because it interrupted the business at hand, which was to bring Frank into a formal relationship with Breuer and the committee. Michael now nominated Frank as art consultant. Colman approved, so did the abbot. Cloud expressed reservations and mentioned Robert Rambusch, but for practical purposes the matter was settled, although we would need another meeting in July to hash over details. Kacmarcik would be our liaison with Breuer on matters artistic, which would turn out to mean every visible detail of the finished structure.

Frank Kacmarcik

Frank Kacmarcik had a longstanding relationship with Saint John's. He was a native of Saint Paul. He first came to Saint John's as a candidate for the lay brothers in 1941. This didn't work out and he left after a year. It being wartime, he was drafted into the army and eventually saw duty in France. In Paris he cultivated his interest in sacred art and began to acquire examples of book art that would become the nucleus of a large and valuable collection. His academic credentials included a four-year diploma from the Minneapolis School of Art and three years of advanced study in Paris. In 1988 he would become a cloistered Oblate at Saint John's, but that was still far in the future when he accepted a faculty appointment in art in 1951.

Frank was single. He had a commanding personality. He had an easy relationship with Abbot Baldwin. His influence on the abbot in aesthetic matters was deep. An exhibit of Marcel Breuer's furniture at the Museum of Modern Art had led him to recognize in Breuer an aesthetically kindred spirit. Without a formal role, Frank critiqued the new monastic wing designed by Breuer and had a hand in such details as the granite wall inscribed with Scriptural and monastic texts in the corridor at the entrance to the sacristy.

Integration of Frank into church planning was a gradual thing. A small group of committee members met on the morning of July 22 to express some reservations about letting him work directly with Breuer. His strongest backers—Benedict, Michael, Godfrey—were not present. The abbot noted some community unease about committing ourselves to Kacmarcik. He thought that an informal arrangement to pay Frank for a specific consultation would be best. Lancelot came to Frank's defense; in the renovation of Saint Boniface Church in Minneapolis, Frank and Bob Rambusch and Frank's former student Gerry Bonnette had argued frequently but came up with a harmonious result.

Jeremy made the sensible suggestion that the committee talk with Frank about his possible role. The upshot of this delibera-

tion was the recommendation that Frank should meet with
Breuer at Saint John's after viewing Breuer's sketches. When
the committee next met with Breuer on August 13, Frank was
present and took an active part in the conversation, and from
there on no one troubled about his contacts with Breuer.

Altar and Baptistery

At this meeting the committee concerned itself with interior
details: the altar, the baptistery, the choir stalls, the pews. Breuer
preferred the main altar to be of white granite to make it stand
out in a relatively dark sanctuary. There was no white granite
in the Cold Spring quarries, so the altar would come from Vermont. How to attach a decorative frontal to the altar on greater
feast days as we were used to doing in the old church came in
for some discussion. This turned out to be a moot point when
rubricists banned such frontals in principle.

Design elements of the baptistery were not yet settled.
Breuer spoke of a square block for the font and the possibility
of screening the sunken area with glass or metal panels. Both
Cloud and Michael objected to the narrow panel of glass running down the center of the high ceremonial door entering the
atrium from the plaza. At one point someone said it might be
nice to have some sculpted figures standing in the open space
over the doors into the nave. Maybe the apostles? This proposal turned out to be a non-starter when someone else asked
whether you would prefer to see them from the rear as you entered the church or as you left.

Window Designer

This was the first meeting where the design of the north
window got serious attention. As yet there was no design. The
question was who might be the designer, and Breuer raised
that question about both of the major artistic elements in the
church, the north window and the apse mural. He suggested
writing to selected artists and offering a fee of $500 to $1,000 for

competition sketches. When we asked who for example might be invited to take part in such a competition, Frank's value as our art consultant was at once apparent. He and Marcel Breuer shared an international field of reference and brought comparable artistic sophistication to the discussion. Cloud knew many of the names but had idiosyncratic tastes. The rest of us mostly listened as this ad hoc triumvirate came up with about twenty names on the spur of the moment, half a dozen or so for the mural, a dozen or so for the window, two or three for either.

A few of the names were familiar. Jean Charlot's chunky religious graphics were popular. Jean Lambert-Rucki's crucifixes were elegant, austere, and not overmarketed. These two were Catholic. Josef Albers and Ben Shahn were not Catholic, although Albers came from a Catholic background, but both were major names in contemporary art. Albers had done the window in the abbot's chapel in the new wing, rectangles in shades of photographic gray with a linear white cross in the center. Breuer mentioned Alfred Manessier, with whose *vernissage* he had become familiar in Paris. Bronislaw Bak, a new faculty member not yet on campus, was not mentioned.

The upshot of this conversation was that Baldwin wrote a letter to Alfred Manessier a week later, August 18, describing the expanse of the window and asking "whether you would be willing to undertake to design this window." Since the abbot didn't have Manessier's address, he sent the letter to the editor of *L' Art Chrétien* with a request that he forward it to Manessier. No doubt Baldwin had talked over this proposal with Breuer, but there was something altogether unsophisticated in the way the abbot went about it. Would you be willing to make 460 sixteen-square-foot stained glass windows? No acknowledgment of the unique scale of the project or criteria for singling out the French artist as particularly qualified to do it. Assurance that Mr. Breuer will look up Mr. Manessier when he gets to Paris completes the effect of a casual business proposition. Three months later the abbot would learn that the letter did not reach Manessier.

Breuer once more put off dealing with objections to clear glass in the side windows. Frank tipped his hand on this persistently vexing question when he observed that stained glass is undesirable at close range. He tended to deliver this sort of sweeping dictum as a decision from the bench that only the artistically uncouth would question.

Blessed Virgin shrine, Confessionals, Cornerstone

Frank was at his best at a meeting two months later when a small group of us—Godfrey, Michael, Cloud, and I—met with him to work through questions about the design of the Blessed Virgin shrine, the confessionals, and the cornerstone. The working drawings indicated where these elements of the complete plan of the church were to be located, but the architect depended on the client to decide what to put in these spaces.

Starting with the Blessed Virgin shrine, we asked ourselves whether it ought to include an altar. Without hesitation we said no. From the first a fundamental principle in planning the church had been that the Christian assembly should gather around a single altar for the Eucharist. Even though there would be close to forty altars downstairs, it was important not to have more than one in the main body of the church.

If there was not to be an altar, then, could the space be used to commemorate sacred artists? An inscription honoring artists devoted to Mary might be fitting. This suggestion was politely received as a passing thought and dismissed.

The chapel would receive natural light through a slit window in the south wall. Frank proposed that this window should be glazed with clear glass and there should be a statue. The statue should be opposite the window and partially screened from the nave. He thought Mary as the Seat of Wisdom would be appropriate. For the present the replica of Our Lady of Montserrat that Abbot Baldwin brought home from Spain could be used. The total effect might be similar to the Chapel of Saint Zeno at Sancta Prassede in Rome or the sixth-century archbishop's chapel at Ravenna.

The two confessionals were at the back of the church, tucked into the wall on either side of the entrance doors from the atrium. This was 1958 and we were talking about standard pre–Vatican II three-section units, with a seat for the confessor in the middle section and a kneeler for persons going to confession in each of the two side sections. The confessionals were to be roomy and to have solid oak doors, not curtains. Frank was concerned that they express what he called the "Seat of Judgment" theme. When the confessional was not in use, the folded doors of the center section were to stand open to reveal a rich and dignified interior, perhaps with an appropriate text or icon above the confessor's seat. The result was to be one of the simplest and finest effects achieved by Breuer in consultation with Frank: a dark oak interior with a bronze-leaf back wall; a generous black leather seat and backrest; the floor raised a step and paved with a tessellated pattern of small black, gray, and white granite triangles cut by a local craftsman.

We talked again about the side windows of the church. Despite Frank's approval of clear glazing, Godfrey objected vehemently that *consecratio* requires enclosure. Frank suggested that one might look out into an enclosed space containing appropriate statuary. The question was not settled.

The cornerstone, a square block of Cold Spring granite to match the exterior stonework of the church, would be laid in another month. John and Paschal joined Cloud, Godfrey, Michael, and Frank for a meeting that evening to give final thought to the design. The stone was to be of the same thickness as the concrete wall in which it would be embedded and to have both exterior and interior faces. Frank would do the lettering. For the exterior face the group approved of dividing the space with a Greek cross and inscribing the Greek initials for "Jesus Christ"—IC and XC—in the upper quarters of the space and the numerals of the year—19 and 58—in the lower quarters. On the interior face the three-letter Greek words for "Light" and "Life" would pivot on their common vowel, *omega*, to form a mystical symbol of Christ. The cornerstone thus designed was laid on November 19.

October–November 1958

XI The committee met with Breuer and Val Michelson on October 2. Val did an overview of construction progress to date and enumerated the next steps. Many of the details were technical and not of great interest in retrospect, but the emergence of Bruno Bak as a possible designer of the north window came as news. The committee had before it a preliminary sketch of a design by Bak for the window. Michelson's summary of the meeting indicates that there was "a generally shared favorable opinion of the sketch," and Breuer expressed satisfaction with the way Bak solved the difficulties imposed by the rigid architectural form. On the whole, however, the committee still favored seeing a sketch by Manessier. Breuer had not yet talked with him in Paris but hoped to see him before the end of the month. Meanwhile Bak should be encouraged to develop his sketch and possibly produce an experimental window in a hexagon that had been poured on the construction site.

Bronislaw Bak

Thus within a month of joining the college faculty, Bak was in the running to do the window. The school paper, *The Record*, for October 24, 1958, did a feature on him: "Polish Refugee Brings Stained Glass Artistry to SJU." John Uldrich, '60, wrote the story. Bronislaw Bak, the new member of the art department, was thirty-seven years old. He was a native of Poland and had spent five years in a German concentration camp in World War II. When freed at the end of the war, he chose to live in Germany rather than return to a homeland under Soviet Communist control.

In Germany he studied art, working in various media, particularly stained glass. He emigrated to America, lived in Chicago, and accepted a faculty appointment to the art department at Saint John's in the summer of 1958. Uldrich's story ticks off the salient points about Bruno Bak's background and gets to the point: "Mr. Bronislaw Bak, Polish refugee who is a new art instructor at St. John's, is working on a design for the stained glass windows which will cover the façade of the new abbey church."

In November Alfred Manessier removed himself from consideration. Writing to Baldwin on November 12, Breuer reported meeting with him. Manessier, seeing the plan for the first time, was hesitant about the hexagonal structure but ventured an estimate of about two years to work out a design and create the window. Breuer thought he demonstrated a good grasp of the architectural importance of the window wall. However, he was not entirely surprised when Manessier sent him a letter the next day pointing out that the "immense banner of concrete" outside would greatly reduce the natural light that gives stained glass its brilliant effect. The concrete honeycomb also posed obstacles to his way of shaping a window. Perhaps the master glassmaker, M. Barillet, should be considered, or Mr. Josef Albers "who has already very successfully executed one of your windows." Breuer sent this information to the abbot in a letter dated November 17. He closed by saying he supposed that "Mr. Bak has continued with his own design which I think is very promising."

Lower Church Crying Room, Relics, Altar

The window was not yet at the top of the committee's agenda. With construction under way, we could no longer put off two minor but vexing questions: where to put a crying room and where to put Peregrin? At a meeting on October 23, Frank offered a guiding principle: the resting place of Peregrin ought to be less of an exhibit and more of a holy place. It might be near an altar. Godfrey was dead set against putting relics in an altar, but as the notion of a separate relic chapel gradually took shape he seemed to change his mind.

The first question, one that had been nagging us since early in planning the parish chapel, was where to put the crying room, that is, a more or less soundproof room from which the parent of a crying baby could view the Mass without disturbing the rest of the congregation. The space between the stairs at the back of the chapel looked like a good location, but the same space looked like a good place for Peregrin. A special altar could be constructed there, accessible to the public yet enclosed in a space separate from the regular parish liturgy. As we talked, this idea gained strength. At some point somebody suggested that other relics might also be displayed in this space.

The abbey had—still has—a large collection of relics accumulated in its early years. In the old church four locally fashioned brass reliquaries in Beuronese style containing several relics apiece were placed on the altar for major feasts. Most of the relics, generally bits of cloth or bone associated with named saints, were never seen but were kept in the sacristy vault in a wide variety of ostensoria, cases, boxes, tins. To the best of my knowledge, nobody had expressed regret that Saint John's lacked a place to display all of them.

Providing such a place was the idea that emerged in this meeting. Frank asked whether we could have a relic room, a place to house all of the relics including Peregrin. It could be lighted by small lamps. There could be an altar. The atmosphere of the catacombs might be evoked. Cloud mentioned the chapel of Saint Cecilia in the catacombs of Saint Callistus. Frank said such a plan would go a long way to counteract Bauhaus influence in the architecture.

We got quite carried away with the concept, dismissed concern about noise from the mechanical room behind the wall, opined that mothers with crying babies could retire to the relic chapel and view the Mass through a grill, or maybe we didn't need a crying room after all. The pastor, Lancelot, principal advocate of a crying room, was not present. In the finished church he would settle for a narrow gallery behind dark oak louvers along one side of the lower chapel; whether a parent with an unruly infant has ever used this peculiarly dark and confined space I don't know. In time it became a handy place to keep folding chairs.

At this meeting we also considered and agreed on a number of guidelines for furnishing and decorating the many small chapels for private Masses. Here again Frank took the lead. He thought the chapels should have an individual character. There could be a variety of crucifixes, candlesticks, paintings, sculptures, tapestries. The altars, all of granite, all of the same dimensions, could be individually designed, some by Breuer, some by Frank or other artists. Cloud urged that the chapels not be overloaded with artwork and that only a crucifix be placed on the wall behind the altar.

We also talked about the main altar in the parish chapel. It would be larger than the altars in the private chapels. Could it be *versus populum*? Probably not if a tabernacle was to be placed on it, but did we need a tabernacle in this chapel? College students would attend Mass upstairs. The parish had Mass at the schoolhouse next to the cemetery on school days. Couldn't hosts remaining after Communion in the parish chapel be carried to the tabernacle in the Brothers chapel? For that matter, there was an increasing emphasis on consecrating only as many hosts as were immediately needed for Communion. All things considered, there was a general feeling that a tabernacle was not needed. Someone added that the altar should be placed so a tabernacle could be added later if wanted. No one caviled at this.

At a later date someone, probably the pastor, decided that there should be a tabernacle on the altar. Consequently, when the church was dedicated in 1961, the altar was not *versus populum*. Still later, in the post–Vatican II liturgical renewal, the tabernacle was removed from the altar to the bush-hammered concrete credence table to one side, and the altar was moved forward so Mass in the parish chapel could only be celebrated facing the congregation.

It was three weeks before we met again on November 14, this time in the art library with most of the committee, including Lancelot, the pastor, in attendance. The abbot opened the meeting by reading Breuer's letter about his recent contact with Alfred Manessier. This was the letter that said the artist could do a preliminary design by April and complete the window in an additional year and a half. Cloud thought a preliminary design shouldn't take that long, and the cost of insuring such a huge window and getting it through customs would be a big obstacle. Frank thought a work of lasting value would be worth the trouble. Lancelot cautioned that when building for the centuries one needed to be patient.

With the pastor present, we went over the questions about the parish chapel again—relic chapel versus crying room, tabernacle or altar *versus populum*. Lancelot thought it was more important to accommodate mothers with small children than the remains of Peregrin, but we reached no resolution. To move the meeting along, the abbot charged Joachim and Michael to study alternate locations for a relic chapel or a crying room. We left the question about the tabernacle undecided and moved on to the baptistery.

Atrium and Apse Mural

Baptistery or atrium? The architect referred to the entrance space as the atrium and kept it windowless except for the clear-glass vertical divider in the main door and the skylight over the baptismal font. The effect was to draw the eye to the church interior, the altar, and the much larger and brighter volume of the nave and choir. The subdued, exaggeratedly plain interior of the atrium was to serve as a muted introduction to the splendor of the worshiping space with its great apse-screen mosaic, perhaps of Christ in glory, and the vast north window, a mystic field of light and color and shadow, though Breuer would not have used those terms.

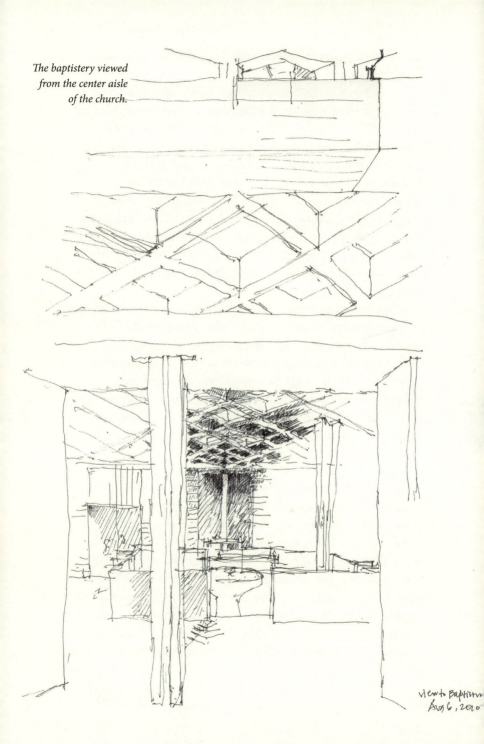

The baptistery viewed
from the center aisle
of the church.

view to Baptism
Aug 6, 2010

Of course, it didn't quite turn out that way. The apse mural, whether of Christ in glory or some other sacred image, which was part of Breuer's conception of the church from his first schematic presentation in 1953, has never been realized. The red curtain behind the screen is a bland background that throws the whole burden of iconic representation on Gerry Bonnette's crucifix above the altar, scaled to a much smaller space, although an improvement over the white plaster corpus that hung there temporarily for the first twenty-five years. What Breuer looked for in the north window may be gathered from his interest in Manessier, an artist who was termed the Rouault of glass for his blocks of deep color framed in dramatic black outline.

For now we were still in November 1958, and Frank had grand ideas for decorating the baptistery. From his remarks at this meeting, I gather that he had not yet discussed the baptistery with Marcel Breuer. He held forth on sculptural ornamentation of the space, a statue of John the Baptist, depiction of the crucifixion or the resurrection or both on a glorious wall. John said it sounded too heavy. Cloud objected to a statue pointing at something. Michael thought Frank was on target. We got into an unusually vigorous and extended discussion with Benedict, Cloud, Frank, and Michael in the middle of it.

Frank was eloquent on the iconographic scheme of the whole church and the importance of this church as a prototype for our time. Sacred art was at the heart of its meaning. He spoke of a tympanum of Christ in glory, a heroic Christ or maybe the saints and Mary on the apse screen. The abbot called him back to considering the font. Yes, the font should be a perfect form, maybe the lid counterbalanced with a dove attached to the cable on which it was suspended. Benedict could see an image of Christ crucified near the font, the resurrection depicted on the glorious wall. Or maybe the Last Judgment, Cloud suggested, and leave the Parousia for the apse screen. Cloud brought this collective flight of fancy down to earth by observing that it would be useful to have a light in the lid of the font.

John added that if running water were wanted in the font, a pipe could easily be run up from the mechanical room directly below.

We talked at some length about baldachins or canopies over the three principal altars upstairs and downstairs. A basic question was whether these symbolic shelters should stand on pillars or hang from the ceiling. Cloud liked a hanging baldachin housing the lighting for the altar. Michael favored a standing baldachin integrated with the altar. Frank suggested a great variety of treatment of all the altars in the church, including the thirty-four in private chapels. At the main altar he thought hanging vigil lights from the baldachin on festal occasions would be expressive of the sacred. If a sanctuary lamp were required, it might also hang from the baldachin. These ideas were advanced; no decisions were made.

There was no time to discuss the Stations of the Cross, but Colman put in a plug for markers on the floor rather than tablets or plaques on the side wall. With that we adjourned for 1958.

January–February 1959

XII With the new year the church began to have a silhouette. The crypt level was enclosed. On top of it a forest of steel scaffolding rose and filled the entire volume of the main floor. A crew of carpenters worked their daily magic on the side walls, measuring and angling and putting in place the wooden formwork that would shape the structure and be permanently visible in concrete.

The planning committee was going to devote lots of time to the north window before 1959 was over, but we didn't know that at the start. An early meeting with Breuer on January 9 dealt mostly with the design of the altars planned for the church, thirty-eight in all. Word from Rome was that our canonist at Sant' Anselmo, Ulric Beste, saw no objection to a solid block altar. We needn't concern ourselves with pedestals if we didn't want them. Breuer said he had thought that many of the private altars in the crypt might be of the same design executed in a variety of materials, but he was quite willing to have some or many altars designed by others.

Artwork in the private chapels was mentioned. Frank Kacmarcik referred to an Alexander Calder mobile of the Trinity. Breuer remarked that he knew Calder and liked his jewelry. He added, "If you tell him what to do, he won't do it. But if you give him an idea of the situation, he may come up with something very nice." The abbot mentioned that Doris Caesar was at work on her statue of John the Baptist.

Breuer described his design for the reliquary chapel and showed us a sketch of the bush-hammered concrete walls, with niches shaped to hold particular reliquaries. For one last time we came back to the crying room and over the pastor's objections agreed on the enclosed side-aisle gallery with room for eight adults. Lancelot wanted a room that parents with children could use from the beginning of Mass; Michael, wearing his liturgist's hat, thought crying rooms should be used only as places of last resort.

Bak Cartoons for Window

The committee didn't meet again until February 25, and then it was to consider six full-size cartoons for the north window prepared by Bruno Bak.

There is probably nothing in writing about Bak doing the window aside from an undated letter to him from the chair of the art department, Cloud Meinberg, assuring him before his arrival that the department had some materials for work in stained glass. Whether the sketch he showed the committee and Breuer in early October simply stemmed from his own interest in doing the window I do not know. Encouraged by the committee's response, he refined the design and circulated it in the monastery around Christmastime. The theme was to be the liturgical year evoked by a non-representational sequence of floor to ceiling panels featuring the seasonal colors.

In those pre-conciliar years missal-toting Catholics were probably more conscious than Catholics are now of the colors of church vestments proper to the liturgical seasons and feasts. I have only the vaguest recollection of the full-scale cartoons, but one with a nice interplay of green and red sticks in my mind. It was pleasantly Christmassy, and the intensity of the pure colors was exciting. The juxtaposition of colors in this cartoon survives in the finished window, but of course it is far from characteristic of the window as a whole, which would be overwhelmingly oppressive if all 486 hexagons were so highly colored.

My notes on the February 25 meeting sound like the continuation of a conversation that began somewhere else and had been going on for some time. We viewed the cartoons in SL3, a large first-floor classroom. Bak was there to present them. Then we moved upstairs to the art department library on the second floor to continue the meeting without him.

The concerns that emerged came down to two: Did the window proposed by Bruno Bak have significant thematic content, and what was the quality of the design? Someone attributed to Bak the belief that the thematic content of a work of art was secondary, that the artist works with love and joy and the result is a kind of universal content that does not have to be defined. At any rate, he was still studying the design and was not ready to present the finished work. However, he could say that he intended to give greater prominence to the paschal mystery than appeared in his original design.

This explanation did not entirely satisfy the group. Someone asked how the window would relate to the iconographic treatment of the apse. Michael reported that he and Godfrey had talked with Bak and told him that if he wanted to incorporate the liturgical year into the window, he should express it clearly and hierarchically. The abbot tiptoed around the edges of the discussion by asking to what extent a patron may suggest changes in a design. He suggested that a small group should meet with Bak and discuss thematic content insofar as such content was desired.

The iffy question was whether Bruno Bak had the artistic skill to carry off this monumental project. Here most of us were on shaky ground. Not so Frank. He flatly stated that he considered the cartoons failures in design—"flat, fragmentary, fluttery," to use his own adjectives. Others wondered whether the artist had lost the scale that he had in the original sketch. Frank was eloquent on the importance of matching the quality of the Breuer architecture. He was not opposed to Bak, he said, but he suggested appraisal of the window by an outside consultant. He mentioned some names: Josef Albers, someone from the Walker Art Center, William Saltzman, then in Rochester, Breuer himself.

John thought that we should trust our instincts with Bak as we had with Breuer and give him the job. Alfred seconded this proposal. The abbot wondered whether we might "endorse" Bak and ask him to proceed without a contract. Colman doubted that we could be more than generally satisfied with the design before the window was completed, but he recommended that we trust Bak's willingness to cooperate. The one concrete suggestion came from Joachim: request Bak to do a larger sketch, perhaps a quarter-scale section of the window. Cautioning that we must not undermine the artist's confidence—whether in himself or us was not clear—Abbot Baldwin undertook to see Bak the next day, expressing full confidence but also providing for continued advice.

With that qualified approval Florian was dispatched to tell Bak waiting downstairs that he could proceed with his work. Given the ambiguity of the committee's language, Bruno Bak could be excused if he thought that he had now been commissioned to do the window. However, in July Benedict was to insist that we had not commissioned Bak to do the window even if he had been told that he could charge orders for glass to the abbey and use as his studio the big dairy barn, standing empty since sale of the Holstein herd in 1956. In September Jeremy was to set straight any of us who thought the committee had not approved the Bak window in February.

Statue, Banner Cross, Private Chapel Details

Before this afternoon meeting adjourned, Frank Kacmarcik brought us up to date on the Doris Caesar statue of John the Baptist. The plaster cast was now completed and awaited our approval. It was eight feet high. Breuer liked it, which Frank interpreted as meaning he considered it suitable for the space. Cloud was still troubled that Caesar was not a Catholic. Frank professed to have stumbled upon her accidentally; the abbot said he had sent her a book and a theological paper by Father Daniel Durken. He assured us—this was the second time—that we were in no way committed to buying the statue.

Finally we were told we had to make a decision now about the cross in the banner. Should it be metal or wood? How big? How mounted? Structural implications dictated making these decisions before work on the banner could begin.

The cross was our first business when we met in the art department library that evening with Ham Smith, Val Michelson, and Bob Gatje. The committee was represented by the subprior and Benedict, Cloud, Colman, Joachim, Michael, and me. It was soon apparent that a metal cross was not much favored. Ham pointed out that bronze or almost any other metal would need to be treated to prevent rain stains on the concrete. He proposed a wooden cross held in concrete arms. An oak cross, he thought, would last about five hundred years. This had monastic appeal, particularly if the oak was to be from our own woods. Should an oak cross be held in place by stainless steel brackets? Ham didn't think so; he preferred plain concrete, but not covered with a mosaic pattern as suggested by Cloud. As for the style of the cross, Colman proposed a Benedictine cross, four arms of equal length like a Maltese cross. This would fit a square window in the banner above the bell platform. Others favored a Latin cross in a rectangular opening, and this configuration won out on a show of hands.

We also considered a range of finishing details about the private chapels in the crypt and the confessionals upstairs, such items as dark-stained cork ceilings, placement of artworks on the side walls rather than above the altars, achieving a baldachin effect with recessed lighting above the altars, warm lighting from gold-washed, recessed lighting in the corridor, dark-stained oak vestment cabinets and drawers, a discreet push button to signal altar servers in their vesting room.

Thinking back on it now, discussion of such details seems trivial until one reflects that it was attention to such details that resulted in the quiet integrity of every part of this great building. It would have been easy to line up the nearly three dozen private altars in so many niches separated by dividers of some sort along the side corridors in the basement. There could have been an acoustical ceiling and an incandescent bulb in a frosted globe over each altar and a crucifix on the wall. The vestments and chalices could have been placed in a centrally located vesting sacristy as in the old church. Breuer took an entirely different approach to this area, no doubt strongly influenced by Frank Kacmarcik. Changing attitudes toward private celebration of the Eucharist have made the thirty-four chapels redundant, but they provide evidence of the architect's ability to integrate structure and art to create a sacred space in the way that he intended on a larger scale in the main body of the church.

XIII

The committee did not meet again until May, but then had two meetings remarkable for what they tell us half a century later about the iconographic richness that Breuer intended in the main body of the church but that largely failed to materialize. The window, of course, was a major element in this plan, and it became the central focus of discussion later in the summer, but the window was not mentioned at all in a long meeting with Frank Kacmarcik on May 7, and it only emerged as one of several topics in a meeting with Marcel Breuer, Ham Smith, Val Michelson, and Frank Kacmarcik on May 27.

On May 7 we touched on the artistic treatment of both of the large chapels in the crypt, the reliquary chapel, the apse screen, and Stations of the Cross both upstairs and down. This was too much to deal with in detail even if we had had detailed proposals to look at, which was not the case.

We started by thinking out loud about the subject matter of the mosaic treatment that Breuer had in mind for the wall behind the altar in the parish chapel. The chapel had not yet been named. Frank now suggested that it be dedicated to the Blessed Virgin and the Brothers chapel to Saint Benedict. The readiness with which the committee welcomed this suggestion tells me that this was not a new idea, but there's no earlier record of it in my notes. Michael now asked what we thought of dedicating the chapel to the Blessed Virgin under the title of the Assumption. Pius XII had defined the dogma of the Assumption of Mary in 1950, so this title reflected current emphasis in Marian devotion.

The conversation that followed seems comical now. How would one represent the Assumption of Mary on the horizontal 33-by-12-foot wall behind the altar? Greater verticality seemed called for. Cloud suggested that the Dormition of Mary would be a more horizontal theme. Since the altar would be centered against the wall and possibly have a tabernacle on it with a

crucifix above it, achieving thematic focus in the center of the
artwork might prove difficult. How about a sort of abstract glory
behind the crucifix, with angels on either side facing the altar?
Or angels on one side and Mary on the other? Or Mary on both
sides under two different titles? Multiple representation of one
person was not uncommon in ancient iconography. We could
have the Immaculate Conception and the Assumption. The subprior said he would prefer the Annunciation to the Immaculate
Conception. Cloud wondered whether the mosaic could be extended to include the side walls of the sanctuary area in order to
catch the light at all times.

At this point Frank reminded us that our job was to decide
content, not design. With this timely reminder we went on to
talk about baldachins versus testers and never got back to iconic
representation of the Blessed Virgin in the chapel dedicated to
her. As for baldachins and testers, in this low-ceilinged space
neither was likely to fit well. In the finished church special treatment of lighting over the altar eliminated the need for either.

What about other artwork in the church? The Brothers
chapel, now named the Benedict Chapel, might have a statue
of Saint Benedict to one side of the altar or perhaps on a metal
mesh screen centered behind the altar. The apse screen upstairs
would have a metal screen as its basic structure, into which
mosaic materials—glass, metal, stone—could be inserted. There
were as yet no artist and no theme for this principal iconographic statement in the Breuer church. Might Louisa Jenkins, a
West Coast artist who had gained attention in 1958 for the first
of her many church mosaics, be the artist, someone asked. By no
means, said Frank, but perhaps we should ask some artists—Bob
Rambusch, for instance—to do sketches. The abbot added that
Frank might do sketches. Frank changed the subject by noting
that Doris Caesar's John the Baptist was now done in bronze and
on exhibit in Boston.

At the end of the evening—we had adjourned for Vespers,
supper, Matins and then returned—we had addressed one topic

of immediate concern and one touchy issue. The topic of immediate concern because of fund-raising was which saints to honor in the private chapels. The abbot and Walter were on the road looking for $5,000 gifts to fund individual chapels, and they wanted to attract donors by linking the chapels with favorite saints. Could we suggest categories of saints that ought to be represented? There were no surprises in our collective response: the Holy Angels, patrons of our congregation; the patrons of our five priories—Our Lady of Guadalupe (Mexico), Augustine (the Bahamas), Maurus (Kentucky), Anthony (Puerto Rico), Anselm (Tokyo); the North American martyrs; the patrons of our own abbots (Rupert, Alexius, Bernard, Peter, Alcuin).

The issue that wouldn't go away but that luckily didn't need to be resolved that night was what to do about Stations of the Cross. In the Assumption Chapel it might be possible to suspend them from ceiling beams on the side aisles. I questioned hanging anything from the ceiling. On the other hand, adopting the opposite approach upstairs by inserting plaques in the brick floor was sure to be controversial and maybe liturgically unacceptable. The subprior said that many of the Fathers objected vigorously to this novel and irreverent proposal. We would certainly need to have the bishop's approval. Frank was in his element with this sort of controversy and gleefully observed that "station," of course, denotes a place, not a picture. We had tacitly conceded that we didn't need the conventional fourteen pictures of Christ on the way of the cross, that numerals would be enough. For now, Godfrey volunteered to consult a Franciscan authority about the propriety of numbered plaques on the floor. Thus entitled to postpone a decision, we adjourned.

Blessed Virgin shrine

Marcel Breuer was with us on May 27 along with Ham Smith, Val Michelson, and Frank Kacmarcik. Breuer was in Minnesota to speak at the Walker Art Center. The committee devoted the afternoon to thinking through the ultimate look of the Blessed Virgin shrine with him and Smith. The area was still inaccessible behind scaffolding: an empty concrete trapezoid with an eight-foot ceiling, a narrow window into the cloister garden, and no side wall to separate the space from movement in the aisle.

We talked about the desired atmosphere: subdued lighting, noble character. Should there be any artificial light? Would natural light and vigil lights be sufficient? Breuer thought provision for lighting fixtures was advisable; they need not be used ordinarily if not wanted, but adding them later if wanted would be awkward and costly. Limit them to ceiling spotlights, not trough lighting.

Treatment of the walls? People kept mentioning mosaic under the influence of ancient examples in Ravenna and Rome. Val Michelson cited the magnificent mosaic interior of the Mausoleum of Galla Placidia in Ravenna. Mosaic walls and ceiling? Too much of a good thing in a small space, said Smith. The concrete window wall was an extension of one of the structural piers bearing the weight of the church. Ham observed that there had been a conscious attempt to leave the structural piers expressive. This reference to one of the secrets of the overall impression of structural simplicity came as a casual comment, but it suggests to me now that Ham had a larger part in the final look of the church than his habitual reserve suggested.

Breuer asked whether we would like to see colored walls, gray, blue, red, gold for instance. Cloud thought a single tone preferable; Godfrey liked lapis lazuli. Breuer thought it odd that we wanted the chapel half-dark but at the same time talked about inscribing texts on the walls.

And so on. By the time the afternoon meeting was over, the major features of the completed shrine had fallen into place. There was to be a perforated screen wall partially shielding the shrine from side-aisle traffic. There would be a single low step up into the shrine. A statue would be centered on the north wall on an axis with the window; Cloud insisted that there was no

instance of off-axis placement of sacred figures until modern
times, although Breuer said he had no problem with an asym-
metrical arrangement. There would be some use of mosaic on
the wall(s) and therefore paving other than brick, since, as Michelson noted, brick floors and mosaic walls don't go together.
There would not be an altar, a baldachin, or granite panels with
texts inscribed on them like the ones in the monastery opposite
the entrance to the sacristy.

Apse Screen

Some members of the committee met again with Breuer and
Smith in the evening to talk about the apse screen and the north
window and add a couple of afterthoughts about access to the
Blessed Virgin shrine.

Comment on the apse screen was sketchy. Smith explained
that plans called for installation of a mesh veil, or more properly speaking a metal grill, from the leading edge of the organ
gallery to the ceiling as part of construction. What to put on
this grill was the question. Our favorite term, "mosaic," was
again in play. The interstices of the grill would be deep enough
to receive a pattern of insets, "like honey in a honeycomb," de-
picting a religious subject. No one expressed a preference for
any particular subject. We came back again to commissioning
or inviting artists to submit sketches showing how they would
exploit the artistic possibilities of this large area. Godfrey asked
whether we might mount a competition, and Colman followed
up by proposing a grant from the Kennedy Foundation to fund
a competition. Frank thought that a theological conference or
two could provide material for artists. In this connection Godfrey cited Jungmann's article in *Worship* on subjects traditional
for the apse. All of this led Breuer to observe that we might
need to wait ten or fifteen years to fill the screen. This in turn
led Frank to say that we might postpone many artistic decisions but not all, lest we be charged with setting up a Calvinistic
meeting hall.

Discussion turned briefly to statuary over the doors leading into the nave from the baptistery. Nothing ever came of this notion, and it's hard to imagine now that we ever gave it serious thought. We had dismissed it a year earlier, but someone apparently still cherished the thought. I suppose it was difficult for all of us to picture a church as devoid of devotional ornament as this one was shaping up to be. Breuer deflected conversation on this topic by suggesting sketches or papers on possible themes for the apse screen and then turning to what he called the most urgent question, how the north window would filter light into the church.

Breuer Reservations About Bak Design

It was on this note that the committee came up against the awkward topic it had avoided since February—the Bak design for the window. Clearly there had been conversations in the meantime, for the abbot now asked, "Will Bak budge, Mr. Breuer?" Breuer's response was oblique. Architects, he said, are used to collaborating with clients. Artists are trained to be independent and original. It was against his—Breuer's—principles to criticize an artist during his work. Besides that, was an artist able to make a change if not convinced of its desirability?

He now offered a measured critique of the Bak design. What he called the inner approach and the main composition he found appealing. Where the design was weak was in combining lines and color into form, especially where the lines were moving. The red, wavy lines representing flame in the central *sursum corda* figure suggested isolation in individual hexagons. The artist's angular lines were stronger. The design was weakest when the composition was not structural. In a small sketch this weakness disappeared, but Breuer thought that in the completed window the wavy elements would look out of place.

Michael asked whether the artist shouldn't experience the building before designing a solution for the window. His question implied postponing a decision about the design of the window and therefore the artist. Breuer granted the point but rejected its application in this case. The glass surface was so important. It would create a great part of the experience of the church. It was probably as important as the architecture itself, he said.

Godfrey came to the defense of curved lines, a matter of artistic integrity as he saw it. Breuer repeated that he suggested an angular approach because the artist's curved lines were weak and faulty. They were not his strength. He did not handle them with high artistic quality. He was better when he was more relaxed, less ambitious, not as rich but superior in quality. Bak's work was not baroque, as he said, but romantic expressionism. As a kind of afterthought he added that he was not sure of Bak's sense of color. The plan was not too dark, but the reds in particular seemed harsh and lacking in depth.

Michael found Bak's symbols dated, clichés as expressions of religious meaning. He referred to trees, streams of water, fish swimming. Had he spoken to Bruno Bak about this? His comment that nothing was changed to date seems to say so. However polite Mr. Breuer might be, Michael thought the artist needed to realize his relation to both architect and client.

The abbot said that he had better have a few people besides himself talk to Mr. Bak, and then he changed the subject to note a recent article in a German periodical claiming that bells need to be housed in a bell-loft to achieve proper resonance. Breuer said that he would make a point of reading the original German, although none of the bell people or Walter Holtkamp or the acoustical engineer had questioned the bell program.

To wind up the evening, we went back to the Blessed Virgin shrine. Some were concerned that it be accessible to monks who followed the old custom of kneeling a moment at the Blessed Virgin shrine on entering the church for morning prayer or leaving after evening Compline. Could comparable access be provided in the new church by widening the doorway to the shrine or substituting a low parapet for a section of the screen wall? Breuer agreed that this could be done.

July 1959

XIV The committee did not meet again until July 20, but then in a series of meetings—July 20, July 27, August 4, September 1, September 3—the topic of the window came to a head. The question was simple, although no one put it so simply: Was Bronislaw Bak to do the north window or not? There were to be seven more meetings between mid-October and mid-December before the issue was finally settled.

The meeting on July 20 was short. Abbot Baldwin, John, Benedict, Cloud, Jeremy, Joachim, Lancelot, and I were present. By now the Bak window enjoyed wide acceptance in the monastic community. Bak had produced a detailed layout large enough to show every piece of glass, and he was turning out completed panels, even though a decision to have him do the window had not been formalized. To avoid acceptance by default, Benedict and others urged that an outside expert on stained glass be called in to critique the design. The abbot was not comfortable with this. He objected that we couldn't do much about Bak's design, that Bak hadn't shown himself receptive to criticism, and that in reality there wasn't much we could do short of scrapping the whole thing. For that matter, what would we do if we got somebody from the Walker and they utterly rejected—his word—Bak's window? To this objection some of us said we thought no critical judgment was likely to be so absolute but that an external critic might be helpful to us, the planners, in making up our own minds about the suitability of the design.

John said he was satisfied with the design as it was. Cloud kept saying what he thought was wrong with it, that it was

neither abstract nor representational but a little of each, that
Bak's theme had changed from the liturgical year to the paschal
mystery, and he, Cloud, particularly disliked the Tree of Good
Fruits that had somehow got into the picture. They disagreed
about what Breuer thought of Bak's work. John recalled that
Breuer's first reaction was favorable. On the contrary, said
Cloud, Breuer did not like Bak's management of color and form
when he first saw the proposed final design in May.

Consultation on Bak Design

Gradually we got around to agreeing to have someone
who knew stained glass come and look at the design. Benedict
mentioned Emil Frei, president of the Emil Frei Stained Glass
Company, Saint Louis. Joachim added William Saltzman, a
Minneapolis artist in his early forties recognized for his work
in stained glass as well as other media. A week later the abbot
called a short meeting after lunch to say that William Saltzman
was willing to come at any time, but Emil Frei was in the hos-
pital and not likely to be available for two or three weeks. The
abbot was to be away part of August, so it would be good to
have someone join Saltzman this week if possible. Were there
other names?

Cloud mentioned Meg Torbert at the Walker Art Center and James Johnson Sweeney at the Museum of Modern
Art. Malcolm Lein was a well-known Minneapolis architect
whose house for Martin Friedman, director of the Walker Art
Center, had drawn particular attention. He was close at hand
and aware of Breuer's work at Saint John's. When contacted,
he agreed to come. Thus it was Malcolm Lein who joined
William Saltzman in critiquing the Bak window in prepara-
tion for a marathon meeting with Marcel Breuer, Bruno Bak,
and the committee on the afternoon and evening of Tuesday,
August 4, 1959.

XV The meeting took place in three successive sessions. The first session took place in late afternoon and brought Breuer together with Saltzman and Lein, Frank Kacmarcik, and committee members John, Joachim, Jeremy, Benedict, Florian, Cloud, and me. The abbot was not present nor was Lancelot. Both of them, as well as Bruno Bak and Val Michelson, would join us for the second session after dinner. For the final session at 9 p.m. the consultants and Bak would not be present, but all the rest of the group would stay until calling it a day at 11 p.m.

At the afternoon session our guest critics summarized their impressions. Both were highly complimentary of the architecture. "Magnificent," Lein called it. Great architecture, he said, should be the house of great art. The question as he saw it was whether the work of art in question was worthy of the building. He distinguished between concept and design. Concept was not his primary concern in this discussion. The design of the window, he did not feel, was of the caliber of the architecture. The development of the glass had proceeded from a small-scale sketch to extremely large sections of the total design, and the unity of the work had not been maintained. It looked to him as if the approach had been to individual hexagons, not the whole window. The result when finished would be nice pieces but not a strong total work.

Saltzman wasn't altogether sure they would be nice pieces. He found the window to be a repetition of many modern clichés. Some individual units were overdone, lacking in simplicity. Things about the overall pattern could be strengthened to give it greater power, but his preference would be for a new work of the same quality as the architecture.

Breuer expressed general agreement with Lein and Saltzman but said he was not dissatisfied with the overall pattern of the window. He would accept the whole composition as such. The forms he thought expressive and appropriate. He had two strong criticisms of Bak's execution of them. One was that whenever Bak went into "ambitious" composition, he erred on color and exuberance, not seeming to understand the kind of restraint necessary in color and individual composition. His other major criticism was that Bak tended to lose his original composition. In pieces already completed his darker panels were now lighter than his light ones in the first sketch. There was reason for concern that the final work would not have color coherence or unified composition and would approach poor art.

The critics and Breuer engaged in discussion. Saltzman thought the big idea was still being experimented with but that Bak was successful with decorative elements. To this Breuer said he had no problem with a decorative window, though "the Fathers" might. He thought Bak's decorative pattern was destroyed by the more ambitious sections of his composition. Lein cited by contrast the sure hand and careful study that must have gone into the 1954 Albers window in the abbot's chapel in the new wing of the monastery and said he didn't see such quality forthcoming in Bak's composition. On a closing note before dinner, Saltzman registered his objection to etching or painting on stained glass. The committee members had sat through this part of the day's historic meeting as attentive listeners.

Bak Joins the Consultation

We reconvened at 6:45. Now Abbot Baldwin, Lancelot, Bruno Bak, and Val Michelson joined us. For some reason Michael Marx was not present for this important meeting, even though his interest in the window and his skepticism about the quality of the Bak window were well known. It is a tribute to Bak, Breuer, and Baldwin that this meeting took place. It couldn't have been a comfortable meeting for any of them, or for Lein and Saltzman.

Abbot Baldwin began politely by asking Mr. Breuer to summarize for Mr. Bak's convenience the criticisms of the window pro and con voiced in the afternoon meeting. Breuer did so in a few sentences without attributing particular opinions to either of the visiting critics. The gist of his comments was what we expected from the afternoon meeting. He found the original sketch attractive. On the basis of full-scale details in the cartoons and the demonstration panels completed by Bak, he had come to doubt the artist's ability to carry out his own design on the vast scale required for the window wall. He repeated his suggestion that Bak's strength lay in the decorative elements of his design.

In an effort to bring the critics into the conversation, Joachim asked Malcolm Lein to repeat his comparison of Josef Albers' window for the abbot's chapel with the Bak design. As he had in the afternoon meeting, Lein distinguished between concept and design and assured Bak that he was not saying what Bak's concept should be. His concern was that not nearly enough study had been done of the intermediate stages between the original sketch and the final window. He complimented Bak on the quality of some hexagons. Nonetheless, his impression was that the total work lacked integration and that "lots" of detailed studies were needed, despite the time it would take to do them.

Bak finally got into the conversation when Abbot Baldwin asked him whether he understood what Lein meant. Bak said, "Yes and no." How could anyone make a critical judgment of the whole work based on one or two hexagons? He defended the unity of the design, citing, for example, the continuity of whites and grays running through several hexagons.

Val Michelson intervened to say that he didn't think that was exactly Lein's point. To make his point about detailed study with an example, Lein asked whether any of us were familiar with Carl Millis' heroic onyx statue of an American Indian in Saint Paul. Millis did many studies of this thirty-foot statue—sketches, models, detailed study. Each successive study showed some change. By contrast the Bak window had jumped from a very small initial sketch to a concept of the completed work, but, he commented, "Concepts are a dime a dozen." Saltzman nodded: the initial sketch lacked almost all detail. One should be able to look at any part of the finished window and see a satisfying work of art, explained Lein.

Bak was having none of this. He was outnumbered in this conversation, but he insisted that he knew what he was doing and was entirely capable of subordinating individual hexagons to the overall plan. Saltzman interrupted him to note the difficulty of competing with the hexagonal pattern. He thought the hexagons tended to be too static. The risk was that the window would be a lot of individual compositions rather than a unified surface of glass. He thought part of the problem was too much etching and painting. Bak disagreed and for a few minutes the two men engaged in a technical discussion of line, glass values, and relative dimensions within a pattern. Lein volunteered that he objected to painting on glass in principle, to which Bak replied that the practice went back to famous examples in the twelfth century.

The critics faulted the "feel" of the design. To Lein it felt old, and he asked whether we wanted an old window in a new church. Saltzman on a different tack questioned whether the window could afford to be "fun" in each hexagon. To his mind, fun had run away with concept in several of the finished hexagons.

By now the conversation had gone on for the better part of an hour, see-sawing between significant but secondary questions. Although no one said so, we had yet to address the central question, which was whether Marcel Breuer approved of Bak doing the window. Breuer drew attention to our reason for meeting by stepping into the conversation with a story illustrating that you can't argue with an artist. He put our situation plainly. We were up against fundamentals, he said, not something you can get over by giving good advice.

About Bak's work he said once more, "I went along very much with the general composition." One sees such large forms

in memory, he explained. "I genuinely liked them." Why had
his appraisal changed? Having seen the full-scale cartoons and
some demonstration hexagons, he was now afraid that Bak
would not achieve his own composition. He loses himself in the
individual hexagons, Breuer asserted. He lacks the discipline to
resist the lure of the glass in the hexagons. "The window, being
so large, is perhaps somewhat above Mr. Bak." "I would prefer an
overall decorative pattern to a composition which tends to be a
religious expression and does not succeed." When Bak attempts
expression he loses discipline. The small composition—the
original sketch—had excellent character. To follow it up in full
scale is a completely different task. (The two sentences in quota-
tion marks are exact quotes. The other sentences in this paragraph are close paraphrases. It didn't occur to anybody to record
the proceedings of the committee at this critical juncture.)

Where do we go from here? asked Breuer. The window is
extremely important in the whole church. Perhaps Bak's original
composition "subdued" could be used. Bak deserved credit for
coming to terms with the building in his original composition.
Michelson added in his favor that Bak had been struggling with
the window constantly.

If more studies were needed, would enlargements of the
original sketch be helpful? inquired the abbot, and attention
again strayed from the central issue before the committee.
There was fragmentary comment on how the kind of studies
recommended by Lein and Saltzman might be conducted. Lein
apologized for compounding the problem for us. Abbot Baldwin
opined that we were all better for having aired the problem; we
were thus anticipating some of the criticisms we would otherwise face later. For the record he recalled that Mr. Bak began
by inviting help. A process of learning had been going on
throughout the planning of the church. Seen from that angle,
this meeting had been most valuable. He thanked Bak, Lein, and
Saltzman for their presence and adjourned the meeting while
they left.

Breuer and Committee Review Critique

The committee reassembled at nine o'clock with Breuer still present and dealt with miscellaneous topics in short order. The standard spacing of pews was two feet ten inches, and that is what it would be in the parish chapel. Upstairs we would go to thirty-six inches on the main floor with loss of one hundred linear feet of seating. As requested by the pastor and former college chaplain, Lancelot, a book rack could be attached to the back of the back pew on the main floor and placed in front of the seating in the balcony. Service books might be placed on shelves underneath the pews. Other items got cursory attention: chapter house seating, a parapet on the bell platform, Stations of the Cross indicated by plaques on the floor, faucets for watering the lawn in the cloister gardens and on the mall in front of the church.

Then it was back to the unfinished business of the window. We were at ease with Breuer. With the visitors gone, it seemed natural to include him in our conversation. Abbot Baldwin started by reporting that Malcolm Lein had suggested to him three possible approaches to our uneasiness about the Bak design. We could (1) release Mr. Bak, (2) have him make further studies under consultation, with the understanding that the window would be his, or (3) allow him to go on as he chose.

Breuer's comment on these three approaches was mixed. He did not discount the value of discussion. It was possible that Mr. Bak would profit from consultation, but he was not a great artist, and at best his work would be decorative. A great artist would retreat from the complexity of Bak's window and provide a simpler design. The glass runs away with him; every piece of glass is pretty against light. We could go into a general pattern with only weak contrasts—but it would probably be like skinning him.

As for releasing Bak, as Mr. Lein so diplomatically put it, Abbot Baldwin put his finger on the basic issue. We would have great practical difficulties and severe repercussions if we discontinued Bak's window. We all knew what he was talking

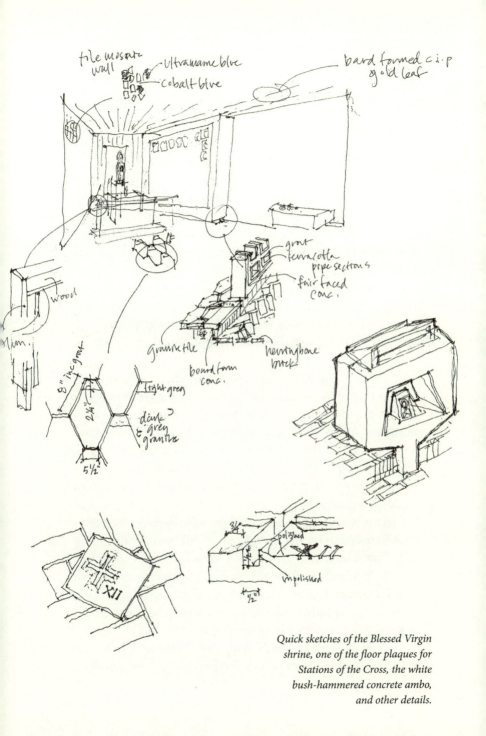

tile mosaic wall

ultramarine blue

cobalt blue

bard formed c.i.p gold leaf

wood

trim

grout terracotta pipe sections

fair faced conc.

granite tile

board form conc.

herringbone brick

3/8" inc grout

2¾"

light grey

dark grey granite

5½"

XII

3/8"

polished

unpolished

1/2"

Quick sketches of the Blessed Virgin shrine, one of the floor plaques for Stations of the Cross, the white bush-hammered concrete ambo, and other details.

about—the way that many in the monastery had identified with
the artist, approved of his religious themes, found his design
beautiful, and approved of his choice of Brothers Adrian Cahill
and Placid Stuckenschneider as assistants, later to be joined by
Brother Andrew Goltz. Work on the Bak window was already
underway. To cancel it would fly in the face of community senti-
ment and also represent a waste of time and money.

What was more, we wanted the window to express a religious meaning. Both Benedict and Florian made this point,
perhaps their only point of agreement on the window. Breuer
hedged on this point. He saw the window first of all as a wall
that filtered light into the church. It might also express an idea,
but from his point of view such a statement was not necessary. In an unusual display of feeling, the abbot swiftly set him
straight: symbolic content of some kind was desired. Trying to
patch over the discordant moment, Lancelot said he thought a
very plain window with obvious symbolism, "a cross or two,"
would do.

Now for the first time someone raised the possibility of asking Josef Albers to sketch a design for the window. My notes
don't indicate the source; it may have been Joachim, who ad-
mired the Albers window in the abbot's chapel and was consistently cool to the Bak design. Breuer recalled a sketch by Albers
that had very plain whites and yellows with a huge cross super-
imposed. Breuer didn't particularly like it, but he thought Albers
could do a good job.

To the best of my recollection, there had been no talk of
an Albers design for the window up to this point, but mention
of his name now was a straw that several committee members
eagerly clutched. Would it be financially feasible to start anew?
asked Benedict. Could we ask Bak to collaborate in producing
a window designed by Albers? asked Breuer. The abbot thought
Bak would not work with someone else.

Would an artist of Albers' stature be willing to have his window produced in a barn on our campus? I asked. Breuer was

sure Albers would be delighted, and an Albers design could
probably be produced much more easily than Bak's, six colors
instead of a hundred. The abbot was leery of Albers, "Perhaps
too cold." He is an experimenter, explained Breuer; he will devote two or three years to exploring gray against white, but his
early work was full of color.

The abbot changed the topic: How many would favor adopting Mr. Lein's second alternative, Bak with consultants? We
hashed over Bak's capabilities once more. No one thought he
would collaborate with another artist, much less produce another artist's work. Yet the subprior stated flatly that because
of repercussions within the community he would not go along
with dismissing Bak.

So what to do? We floundered awhile, touching on strategies
already rejected, then in the end gratefully approved Florian's
proposal to postpone action on the window until the hexagon
wall was completed. The panels already done by Bak could then
be put in place and judged *in situ*. If work on the window were
terminated now, Florian thought that Bak might leave and the
effect in the monastic community would be bad. Could Bak be
commissioned to do some small windows elsewhere while work
on the church window was suspended? Breuer queried. The
abbot preferred a more immediate approach. Ask Bak to restudy
a specified section of his design in line with today's criticisms
until we could get a sketch from Albers, then ask the two of
them to collaborate if we preferred the Albers design.

Somehow that seemed like a splendid idea to all of us, even
though it flew in the face of our earlier opinion that Bak was an
unlikely prospect for collaboration on anybody else's design. The
meeting had gone on well beyond the bedtime of the monastic
members, who were expected to get up at 4:45 a.m. for Prime,
the Little Hours, and the conventual Mass. Maybe we were
also groggy from confronting an intractable issue since mid-
afternoon. Whatever the explanation, we parted on a little swell
of euphoria. Val Michelson would counsel Bruno Bak to restudy

his design in line with today's recommendations. We would await an alternate design from Josef Albers. We agreed with Mr. Breuer that Mr. Bak had been handled more than fairly; he had been given every opportunity to respond to criticisms of his work. Even so, we agreed not to mention any names until we had sketches from Albers to compare with Bak's design.

September 1959

XVI The committee did not meet again in August. Construction of the hexagon wall went ahead steadily. The hexagons were poured in halves in metal forms on site, then cemented in place so smoothly that the joint was virtually invisible. The abbot was away. In consultation with Val Michelson, Bruno Bak reconsidered some elements in his design. Josef Albers was asked whether he would consider submitting a design.

Against this background the committee met twice in the first week of September, the subprior chairing the meetings. All of the committee except the abbot, Benedict, and Colman were present at the first of these meetings on September 1. The subprior wanted to discuss a letter from Albers received that morning. Albers wrote that he was eager to do the window. His preliminary fee would be $1,500–$2,000. He thought it would be possible to produce the window at Saint John's. Breuer had advised him to avoid coldness in the window. He was thinking of a text like "Sanctus" with symbols and warm colors—yellow, orange, red.

The question immediately became whether we were interested in continued correspondence with Albers in view of the satisfying results of Bak's reworking of his design in the last month. The subprior had seen Bak's latest work and was impressed. He reported that Val Michelson was also generally favorable, with the caution that proof would come only in actual glass. Should we then still request an Albers sketch, or should we assume that Bak could do the job and let him go ahead? As an aside, the subprior observed that he did not like Albers' ideas about the window.

Lancelot emphasized the improvement in Bak's design. Godfrey said that he was "permanently opposed" to Albers because he lacked religious faith. Albers was a *technician*. Godfrey had been won over by a visit to Bak earlier in the day. Bak showed him a window he had done for Msgr. Reynold Hillenbrand. Godfrey thought Bak's design for the church window represented "a very valid general theme," and he was very satisfied with Bak.

Jeremy erupted into one of his rare but always memorable speeches. In his former career he had been a trial lawyer, and he prided himself on being plainspoken. He corrected Godfrey and others on a number of points about which they were in error. The gist of his argument was that no one had objected to Bak's original sketch way back in February, and there was no reason to consider another artist now. Period.

Despite the clarity of Jeremy's position, I summoned up all my courage as the junior member of the committee and asked whether we could gracefully withdraw from communication with Albers quite so abruptly. Excited discussion ensued. Jeremy himself granted that Bak's scale drawing did not equal finished work. Perhaps it would be advisable, someone volunteered, to stay in touch with Albers until we saw the results of Bak's modified design in some completed work.

Both the subprior and the treasurer, Florian, thought that we shouldn't spend $1,500–$2,000 if we didn't need to. Cloud and Joachim felt that this sum was not too much to pay for having an alternative at hand in case Bak's design was ultimately rejected. Jeremy wondered when the money to Albers would be due. Florian thought that we must pay Albers for time devoted to the project whether or not he produced a finished sketch, but he wasn't clear what financial arrangements had been made.

Both Florian and Alfred were ready to tell Albers to forget about the window. Others collectively urged that we go slow in light of what they saw as errors in our previous procedure. Alfred objected to pressure put on the committee by Breuer. Discussion became mired in inquiring where our procedure had gone wrong. It was just as well that we had to adjourn for Vespers without deciding anything.

Committee Agrees to Request Albers Sketch

We met again on Thursday, September 3, at the same time and with the same members present plus Benedict. The question was still whether we should request a sketch from Albers. After Tuesday's meeting it was easy to identify fans and critics of Bak in the committee. Alfred, Florian, Jeremy, and John were stalwart supporters of Bak. Godfrey was a recent convert to Bak but was known to be prey to sudden enthusiasms. Benedict and Michael preferred a wider choice, and for the moment that meant encouraging an Albers entry in the field. Since there was as yet no Albers design, making an argument in its favor came down to noting the artist's undoubted stature and the likely saving if we proceeded with a design that would in all likelihood be much simpler than Bak's. Cloud and Joachim leaned toward the Albers side, if only because both had serious reservations about the artistic quality of Bak's work. Without much artistic sophistication, I sympathized with their view and favored seeing what Albers had to offer. Lancelot professed to be independent, although he said he didn't see what was wrong with Bak's design.

The discussion was again free-ranging but without the note of irritation that marred Tuesday's meeting. There was lots of repetition, but there were also one or two new notes. On a quarter-million-dollar project, Benedict submitted, looking at two alternatives would seem to be a prudent minimum. He added that a design by Albers, even if not used, would be an asset in the art department. Countering this train of thought, John considered it a foregone conclusion that Breuer would prefer an Albers sketch and we would have a hard time getting him off it.

As for the religious quality of the work of the two artists, Benedict made the point that demonstrated competence is the only reason for faith in an artist. So far Bak looked more like a student than a master. He might well do a decent window. Albers might do a masterpiece. It was quite possible that he would do a superb religious work. To this Michael added that a document on sacred art from the Holy See called for Catholic membership on planning committees but skill and the ability to express religious feeling in artists. Florian asserted that Breuer had no religious feeling coming as he did from the materialistic Bauhaus. Cloud warned against pat generalizations. Benedict said the spiritual quality of the church had to come from us, not the architect.

Aside from this exchange, the meeting was free of argument. At one point Lancelot asked Cloud and Joachim to explain what was wrong with the Bak window. Joachim replied that he didn't want to judge the Bak window, but he might mention some of the criticism offered by Lein and Saltzman. In Bak's defense, he added, the man's teaching load was too heavy to allow enough time for work on the window. We might recall, however, that Bak himself had said he knew nothing about symbolism. Joachim thought the obvious thing to do now was to get an Albers sketch and ask qualified critics to judge which was better.

Joachim was good at serious listening. Long stretches of discussion could go by without a word from him, but when he offered a comment it was likely to be thoughtful and clearly put. His comment now led Alfred to move that we reaffirm what he described as our resolution of August 4, that Bak continue his execution of forty hexagons and that Albers be invited to submit a design. In a bow to procedure, John, the chair, called for a vote and got eight in favor and two opposed. That took care of our purpose in meeting, but there were several suggestions about helping

Albers get the religious thing right: a glorified cross, rays of light from a hidden source. Perhaps he could be sent the titles of some instructive books or maybe just one book, Louis Bouyer's *Paschal Mystery.* Alfred thought all of this too complicated, that all Albers needed from us was a simple answer that, yes, we wanted him to do a design for the window. We let it go at that.

The subprior closed the meeting by reading a letter from Breuer covering various details of his last visit.

October 7–November 11, 1959

XVII We now had a bit of a breather from the window. Two important meetings took place, one on October 7, another on November 11, dealing with a wide range of settled details. Looking at my notes now, I can see the interior features of the church coming together in their final shape and texture. Yet we were still tentative on many points, and some of our concerns, though understandable in 1959, now seem quaint. I don't know, for instance, that anyone considered covering the communion tables with a cloth once we moved into the church. Remarkable about the communion tables is that they were so soon outdated for Communion but proved useful as stands for floral arrangements at funerals and reliquaries on All Saints Day.

Val Michelson and Frank Kacmarcik were with us at the October meeting. Abbot Baldwin was not with us. Frank had just come from New York. The Doris Caesar statue of John the Baptist was finished. Frank said it wasn't what one expects, but he thought the scale and volume were quite good and nicely suited to its intended location. What did he mean, "Not what one expects"? Well, Frank said, you wouldn't stop and kneel before it. It wasn't sacred art in that sense. But it was, he thought, deeply religious. He added that photographs didn't do it justice, so he hadn't brought us any photos. The subprior reminded us once more that we were not committed to buying the statue. Frank said it would ordinarily cost $7,500, but we could have it for $2,500, and Caesar didn't expect a decision until the statue was tried in place. The $2,500 included shipping.

Breuer had now completed almost all interior details, reported Frank. The baldachin was very simple. It hovered in space, held by a network of silver cables. Lights for the altar and speakers for the choir and nave would be housed in it. It could be of wood or metal and might be white or colored, whichever would relate better to the apse mural behind it.

The altar itself would be of white granite. Should the communion tables match it? Lancelot thought the materials should be the same. More important, should the baptismal font be of the same stone as the altar? Breuer preferred black granite for the font to match the floor of the baptistery and to emphasize its function as a pool. How the font was to be drained was a question yet to be resolved.

Some questions about sanctuary furniture were settled on the principle that everything in the new church should be as simple and unobtrusive as possible. Shelves attached to the front of the choir stalls would do as credence tables. No platform was needed at the ambo. Chairs would do when rubrics called for ministers to be seated during the liturgy. No swing-out desk was needed at the acolytes' place in choir.

The final topic was whether to purchase a New Mexican *santo* that Frank saw in New York. Purchase price was $450. The subprior asked whether the committee would prefer to postpone considering this question until the abbot's return from Europe. Most of us thought that would be wise. I objected to the committee's deciding on individual works of art for the church. Frank noted that the abbot had spoken of allowing $500 a chapel for decoration. Michael gently reminded us that we were not art museum curators, and thus the meeting ended.

Looking across the seating in the main body of the church toward the recently created Blessed Sacrament chapel and the east cloister garden, the leading edge of the balcany to the left, the altar and choir stalls to the right.

Holtkamp Visit

In mid-November we had two big meetings on successive days. On November 11 Marcel Breuer and Ham Smith came out from New York. Walter Holtkamp, the organ builder, joined us from Cleveland. Charles McGough, the contractor, sat in on the afternoon segment of the meeting for the only time in the five-year history of the planning committee. Val Michelson and Frank Kacmarcik were present, along with the full committee membership chaired by Abbot Baldwin. The meeting took place in the upstairs sacristy space of the new wing, where there was room to spread out working drawings of the apse screen, the organ gallery, the baldachin, the communion tables and lectern, the Blessed Virgin shrine, the baptistery, the Saint Peregrin and reliquary shrine, and the chapter house interior. The meeting started at 1:15, broke from 5:30 to 8:15 for prayers and supper, and continued until 11.

We walked through the architect's treatment of the shrines and addressed a few final details. How much of the relic of Peregrin should be visible? Not much, said Kacmarcik. The altar: put magnets on all four sides to attach frontals on great feast days, said John. This was never done. The communion tables with their white granite *mensae* to match the altar: they need to be "monumental," said Breuer; a certain heaviness and solidity is necessary amid such large plastic forms. He did not mention that he had gone beyond mere function to give them a sculptural character interesting in itself.

There were questions about the gospel lectern, the ambo. Was it too close to the fourth communion table? Need it be so prominent? Would it be adequately lighted? There were not enough questions about the baldachin, or rather the sound system to be housed in it. The baldachin would be suspended seventeen feet six inches above the floor of the sanctuary. Two slender speaking tubes over the altar would connect to microphones in the baldachin. Discreetly camouflaged speakers in the leading edge of the baldachin would amplify the voice of ministers at the altar and the ambo, where there would be two more speaking tubes.

As I have noted, I wonder now why we didn't question the adequacy of this system for a space seating nearly two thousand people. As it was, the only question we raised about the balda-chin was the abbot's query about whether the cables holding it in place would interfere with viewing the apse mural. Breuer as-sured him the thin silvery cables would enhance the view of the mural, not block it.

The apse mural was a major topic of discussion. Walter Holt-kamp was with us because the apse mural was also to serve as an organ screen, but of course there wasn't as yet a mural to con-sider. We still did not have an artist to create this work or even to tell us what challenges an artist would face in trying to make a mosaic of high artistic quality by filling only a fraction of the interstices in a big grid. For now Breuer and Smith explained the grid itself. It would be a great rectangle, almost square, forty feet by thirty-two feet six inches, suspended from the bottom edge of the last of the folded concrete trusses that formed the ceil-ing. It would reach down to the edge of the organ gallery but for acoustical reasons hang about a foot in front of it. Ham Smith called this a "floating" effect. The material was cast aluminum and the interstices rectangular and quite small, something like one by two inches.

There were two critical questions about this structure, one artistic, one acoustical. The acoustical question was whether this grid with a mosaic worked into the interstices could also serve as an organ screen. Breuer didn't want the visual focus of the apse to be an organ case. Holtkamp accepted Breuer's reasoning, but he didn't want to put his organ behind a sound barrier. He thought that blocking as much as 30 percent of the interstices would not interfere with the organ if ample space was left open on either side of the screen and at the bottom. Breuer had no objection to glimpsing pipes and wind chests through the 70 percent of the screen that was not to be blocked, nor did he object to glimpses of the works from either side of the screen.

Whether Holtkamp was entirely happy about this arrangement was hard to tell. At one point in the meeting he and Breuer stepped aside for a moment's private conference. Otherwise he was largely silent. His manner, at least in his rare visits to Saint John's, was even more reserved than Breuer's. Two summers later when the organ was in place and he came to superintend its final voicing, he moved around to listen to it from various places. Standing in the west side aisle near the Blessed Virgin shrine in the late afternoon sunlight, he approved the clarity of a classic five-stop registration. After he went home, word among the organists was that he was quite happy about the instrument.

The organ works occupied the center half of the gallery. To either side was seating for private prayer behind aluminum mesh screens that provided both privacy and a one-way view of the altar and sanctuary. The wall behind this seating area was concrete block, the only use of this material in the upper church. Cloud asked whether this plain building material ought to be covered with something more presentable, say paneling or tile? Lancelot seconded Cloud's concern. Breuer said he would experiment with solutions once the church was finished. When the church was finished we found that the wall had been painted a neutral gray and was otherwise undisguised.

Chapter House

The last issue on the agenda of this long and substantive meeting was the interior of the chapter house. Here the drawings called for a sort of UNESCO floor plan, with a semicircular seating arrangement facing a massive, bush-hammered concrete desk elevated two feet six inches above the floor. Three high-backed wooden chairs behind the desk were provided for the abbot, prior, and subprior. Behind them was a bush-hammered concrete wall seven feet high screening the entrance to the room.

We were accustomed to the formal style of chapter meetings, where the abbot, flanked by the prior and subprior, presided from a chair on a simple wooden platform at the head of the room, so no one objected to the same grouping in the new chapter house. But was it really necessary to seat the abbot so much higher than the chapter members? And in fact wasn't the whole concrete structure rather a formidable barrier between the abbot and them? Father Ronald Roloff had written a paper on the tradition of the monastic chapter house which we had all read. He emphasized the paternal, Christlike, even in a certain sense intimate role of the abbot in relation to the Chapter. Stimulated by Ronald's treatment of the subject, Benedict had asked at our October meeting whether the position of the abbot in the proposed chapter house had been re-studied. At that point Frank said it hadn't been.

Now in November I spoke up to say that some members of the community had asked me to register their objections to the plan, particularly the high concrete desk, which they feared would have just the opposite effect from what Ronald described. The monks would be an audience, not a deliberative body. I said I would like to see an alternate sketch without the concrete breastwork but with provision for a table or a prie-dieu for the abbot.

Not everyone agreed. John had no problem with the design. The abbot said he thought we would get used to the concrete desk. Breuer said the elevation was necessary if monks in the back rows were to see the presiding officer. He gave quite a fine talk on the concept of the "chapter house." He granted that the massive desk was not necessary but thought an unwanted United Nations effect could be avoided in the total arrangement of the room. For example, he would like to use stained glass in the dozen hooded skylights.

A related concern raised by Ronald's paper was where to place the *maiestas*. According to Ronald, it was customary to indicate the sacred character of the chapter house by placing a large crucifix or an image of Christ in glory—hence in "majesty"—on the wall behind the abbatial throne or opposite it. I suspect this was news to most of us. There was a crucifix on the wall behind the abbot's chair in the chapter room, but it would have been hard to find a room without a crucifix in the whole place. Having one in the chapter room was not distinctive.

Colman cautioned us not to exaggerate Ronald's observations about designating the sacred character of the chapter house, although he had no quarrel about finding a spot for a Christian symbol. Ham Smith suggested that the *maiestas* be placed on the back wall, where it would be seen on entering the chapter house. The abbot and Cloud both preferred putting it on the wall behind the abbot. But that wall was not much higher than the chairs in front of it. It did not reach to the ceiling. Joachim thought two locations, one at either end of the room, would sufficiently indicate the sacred character of the room. Not to be outdone in piety, Godfrey favored three locations, one behind the abbot, one in front of his desk, and one at the opposite end of the room.

The committee had become comfortable with this sort of free-ranging conversation about theoretical topics in the course of three years. And this discussion was theoretical. Unlike the window, no design for a *maiestas* was in the works. The whole idea was novel and attractive. Discussion could have gone on longer if the hour hadn't been late. Report that excavation for the chapter house was underway gave us a nice solid note on which to close.

Brothers Chapel

The next morning a few of us met informally with Breuer and Smith at eleven in the monastic lounge. The topic was mostly the Brothers chapel. All of the monastic choir stalls had been widened by two inches. This cut the number of stalls in the Brothers chapel from 104 to 96. This was still a greater number than were needed for the lay brothers or for other groups that we could envision using the chapel. The Blessed Sacrament would be reserved in this chapel. Should there be a communion rail? Should there be a baldachin over the altar? Should the organ pipes be exposed? Should there be some sort of iconographic presentation?

All of these questions were noted. If a communion rail was needed, it should be short and off center toward the gospel side of the altar. We decided none was needed. Treatment of the ceiling above the altar would single out the altar adequately without a baldachin, for which there was scarcely room. Breuer preferred to screen the organ pipes with a wooden grill behind the altar. Nothing was said about sacred art or iconographic enrichment.

November 12–25, 1959

XVIII On the next day, November 12, the full committee met with Josef Albers, who had come out from New Haven to present his design for the north window. Abbot Baldwin chaired the meeting. Marcel Breuer, Hamilton Smith, Val Michelson, and Frank Kacmarcik joined us.

Before we gathered in the art library at 1:15, Albers had mounted his sketch on an easel and covered it. There was a genial hum of conversation before the abbot called the meeting to order. Some of the members of the committee had chatted with Albers the night before. Whether it was his German accent or his age, he seemed quite comfortable in our midst. At seventy-one he was at least a generation older than everyone else in the room, including Breuer and Abbot Baldwin. He had retired from chairing the department of design at Yale the year before but remained active as a Yale fellow and was long since internationally known for his work in color and design.

The abbot welcomed Albers and called on Breuer to intro-
duce the topic. Breuer said he had discussed the design with
Albers in New York, and he thought it would be best if Albers
himself explained his thinking on the window before showing
us his sketch.

Albers addressed us as the professor he was, but in language
that was homely, familiar, sometimes humorous. He invited
questions as he went along. Shortly after he started speaking,
Benedict brought in a tape recorder. The recording survives in
the abbey archives. Unfortunately something went wrong—possibly someone moved the microphone—and after the first fifteen
minutes the tape is unintelligible. Thus the charm of Albers'
approach and the clarity of his thinking survives in only a frag-
ment of his whole presentation. The gist of his thought is the
best I can reproduce from what is clear on the tape and my own
notes.

One starts with the conditions of the structure, he said, and
then asks whether the resulting concept fulfills architectural and
theological desiderata. In this case the geometric pattern could
be read in various ways. Hexagons create a distinctive condition.
They don't lend themselves well to vertical or horizontal lines
but connect best on slanting lines. The slanting angles easily
suggest rays and an unlimited field only accidentally cut by the
frame of the building.

Now he uncovered his sketch and pointed out to us that
most of the lines were continuous through the hexagons and
that he had not anchored them in the perimeter of the window.
Instead, the perimeter spaces were clear glass or, as he put it,
open glass at the skyline and the foundation. This was to give
the design a weightless effect and to allow everything to relate
to one basic center "as a parallel to your philosophy." I believe
this was as close as he came to referencing religious symbolism.
All five hundred hexagons—he stopped to ask if that was the ap-
proximate number and Val Michelson said yes. All five hundred
hexagons were "under the direction of this discipline."

Acknowledging the symmetry of the design in response to a leading question from Cloud, he said that was because symmetry is holy, asymmetry individualistic and additive. Perhaps recognizing that this apodictic formula might be questioned, he added, "I like to have a reason for the order." Poking fun at himself, he laughed, "Too German! Too much German stubbornness!"

He talked at length and enthusiastically about his colors. Unlike structure and line, when it comes to color there is no reason but preference: "Gentlemen prefer blondes." Good-natured laughter. "Some people like Pepsi, some Coca-Cola. As Father Cloud knows from last night, I don't like either." He had excluded all blues and greens and what he later called "cement," referring to grays and black. The middle of the window was the lightest and strongest in color, "a sun color suspended." It was "unusual to have in a window so much white." From this "central light" only warm colors emanated: amber, gold, rose. No "cement." "We want to make it weightless, the whole central symbol weightless."

He talked about the characteristics of glass, used some samples to show how light can move with the spectator, showed a series of studies of the same basic pattern, a white or amber cross on a field of alternating waves of color. He would use ribbed white glass to catch extra light, "that extra sparkle." The window should capitalize on light at any time—twilight, moonlight, night illumination. Mentioning artificial lighting led him to remark that he preferred natural light: "The sun and moon are cheaper."

It was an engaging and fascinating lecture. When it came to construction, he said, five-foot hexagons were somewhat dangerous in glass. The windows would need to be stiffened with stainless steel, but there was no reason why the window could not be made at Saint John's. Less expensive than New York. He would want to have his agent on site to supervise the work.

Discussion went on until nearly four o'clock. Breuer's contribution was significant. Originally he planned to paint the

interior of the church white, he said, but it would be left in
natural concrete, since it had turned out well. The floor would
be of brownish-red brick, the furniture dark brown. There were
to be no large colored surfaces other than the window. He was
pleased with Albers' design for both its religious and its architectural content. It complemented the architecture. It retained
its power in small sections, yet every part had reference to the
whole composition.

Breuer's reference to the religious content of the design
sparked comment. Someone—probably Michael—said it could
be viewed as both a resurrection and a Pentecost window. Benedict liked the simplicity of the symbolism. A symbol should not
require an elaborate explanation, he said. Albers achieved simplicity, yet great significance, in his design.

The tape recorder was turned off and we broke for coffee.
When we resumed meeting, it was without laymen other than
Frank Kacmarcik. The merits of the Albers design were not the
topic of immediate concern. The topic of immediate concern
was what to do about the Bak window. Abbot Baldwin did not
think it wise to act on the Albers window at once. He favored
taking time to think it over. Scrapping the Bak window would
be costly; Florian estimated that we had already spent about
$20,000 on it. If we were now to choose the Albers window, we
would need to go to the Chapter for the money to pay for it.

Godfrey and others agreed that we should not make a hasty
decision. For one thing, the whole community should have an
opportunity to consider the Albers design. Benedict thought it
would be good to have Albers talk to the whole community, or
at least the Chapter. Discussion was random, partly about the
cost of not continuing the Bak window, partly about the content of the Albers design. Florian estimated that stained glass
for Bak's window would run to $60,000, with another $55,000
for metal frames and storm windows. Michael observed that if
we put in a bad window, we would continue to pay for it for a
long time. He thought the Bak window said nothing. John said,

what about the *sursum corda*? Michael said he understood Bak took that over from another window, and Bak's design was eclectic.

Behind this discussion the unspoken question was how the community would react to dropping Bak. The abbot finally said it: We have got ourselves into a situation where we have to move carefully out of respect for others' feelings. John favored the simplest solution. He had consistently thought that the Bak design was good and we should stick to it. Others found this too simple. Joachim put it plainly: Both windows say something, but Albers says it well and powerfully, Bak in many words weakly. The difference in quality is all-important. He thought any immediate fuss about dropping Bak would die down.

By now we were looking for somebody to take the burden of decision off our backs. Couldn't we get critics to come in and give us their opinion of the Albers window? What about Emil Frei, who had regained his health, and Malcolm Lein? Godfrey and Cloud especially favored doing this. No one was opposed, but some asked whether Marcel Breuer shouldn't be making this decision? In fact, were we legally free to install a window he did not approve of? Jeremy assured us that we were legally free to put in the window we wanted but noted that in practice Breuer had insisted on approving every detail. John thought it would not be a bad idea to put Breuer on the spot, as though the architect hadn't already quite clearly indicated his opinion of both designs. There was general approval of the abbot and John meeting with Breuer privately and getting his frank opinion of the Bak window.

Before adjourning for Vespers we noted and approved reducing the number of upper choir stalls to 186.

Emil Frei

A week later, November 19, the committee met with Emil Frei. Abbot Baldwin chaired the meeting. John and Benedict were not

present. Val Michelson represented the architect. The topic was
Frei's critique of the two designs for the church window. He was at
ease and explicit in his criticism of both designs. He prefaced his
criticism with the observation that he didn't know why an architect of Breuer's superb judgment was allowing the client to decide
this critical question. The two windows in question were in totally
different artistic realms, totally different squares of reference.

Bak's window was bombastic. It lacked reserve. It used too
many words for what it said. It was the kind of thing that happened early in modern design. The tone of this church should be
Benedictine, not Jesuit, he said. The architecture was monastic.
There was not a wasted line. It was boiled down to the essence.
Having said this, he granted that the glass was charmingly chosen in the panels Bak had completed, and most people would
like it very much if installed.

By contrast, Albers' approach was beautiful and much closer
to the spirit of the church. Maybe it was too cold, too empty,
but of course the sketch, which was all we had to look at, was
not the final word. It was good design. If this were a building of
only ordinary merit, the quality of the window wouldn't matter
too much, "but the church you have here there can be very few
of." Everything that goes into it, Frei said, must be very near the
top. Albers has complete harmony between the glass and the
grid. However, there is not much content. The cross contributes
little to the design and could be thrown out. The window is not
religious; it does not tell a story. In this church that is not important; the story will be told at the altar.

Toward the end of the discussion that followed, Frei qualified his remarks with an important reservation. He did not
want to say that Albers was the final solution. We might prefer
a richer design. What he, Frei, had said was that Albers' design
would be right for the building.

Other points had come up in discussion. Michael tried to
convince Frei that Albers' window was not devoid of symbolism.
What Michael had in mind was the positive force of the design

itself and Albers' use of light. Frei countered that the window was only part of the church and that mystery—what calls for search— was at the other end of the church, apparently referring to the altar or the intended apse screen. Later he responded to Abbot Baldwin that he had no objection to a purely abstract design.

Joachim wondered whether ribbed glass, touted by Albers for its sparkle and economy, would work the way Albers said it would or might direct great beams of light in certain directions. He thought the danger with Albers was that he might simplify things too far.

Lancelot wanted to know whether the average person would object to the Bak window. Frei said he had come here wanting to approve of Bak's window. The average person, he said, has an elephant's hide when it comes to design, but you didn't build this structure to please the average person. The bare concrete will be called ugly, yet it is thoroughly honest, structurally beautiful, Benedictine, Catholic. Reserve and the proper use of lines and materials make the church beautiful.

What about Catholic? Michael asked. Frei responded that if we wanted a warm religious statement, we should not have accepted the hexagonal grid with its confining pattern. Val Michelson said that Breuer had substituted the hexagonal grid for an earlier pattern of varied reinforced concrete rectangles in order to gain greater structural depth in this freestanding wall. Frei said we would get bad art if we asked a non-believer to do an involved theological theme that he could not believe in. In this very simple design religion made no difference. Even athe- ists believe in light. Frei himself would prefer to have Catholics do Catholic churches when competent, but non-Catholics some- times brought a fresh view to Catholic subjects.

Frei's parting advice was that if we went ahead with the Bak window, in ten years we would be awfully sorry, but we should consult a few more people. Experts, he said, were a dime a dozen. If we got three or four similar opinions, we could be pretty sure we had the real story.

This was a Thursday. We had a short meeting at 4:45 on the following Tuesday, November 24, to ask ourselves whether we wanted to follow Emil Frei's advice to call in more experts. Abbot Baldwin was not present nor was Godfrey. The question was whether we should invite Malcolm Lein to come back and give us his opinion of the Albers design.

In a meeting chaired by John Eidenschink, who had advocated going with Bak from the start, and including Florian Muggli, who as business manager constantly reminded us that selecting anyone else would require chapter authorization of the required expenditure, the outcome was predictable. We had heard Lein in August; why bother him again? Alfred thought Frei's visit had been most helpful; Florian thought fifty experts, fifty opinions. I said either Bak or a moratorium, but in any case postpone Lein's visit until the community's feelings could be consulted. How I thought this might be done I don't recall.

There was a little discussion about observing poverty by not spending money we didn't need to spend, and we finally voted four in favor of Lein's visit and six against. We then agreed that we should vote on the window soon and tentatively set a meeting for 3 p.m. the next day.

Decisive Vote

The next day, November 25, was a Wednesday. The committee gathered at three in the monastic lounge—in later years called the Abbot's Parlor. Eleven of the twelve members were present: Abbot Baldwin, Subprior John, Alfred, Benedict, Cloud, Colman, Florian, Godfrey, Hilary, Joachim, Lancelot, and Michael. Jeremy was not present.

Baldwin chaired the meeting. He approached the topic from a characteristically oblique angle without actually saying what the topic was. He was glad that we had agreed to have a meeting. A definite decision soon would be best for all concerned. The committee was to be complimented for meeting many past problems efficiently and smoothly. The present problem was unique. We would not have the same problem with the apse screen.

With the apse screen he was on neutral ground, and he went into some detail. Breuer was eager to have sketches of the screen from various artists soon. Ben Shahn and Gerry Bonnette had been mentioned. Rucki was a possibility, although Breuer was hesitant about him. There were some artists in Barcelona whom Baldwin had met and others at Montserrat whom he had heard of. Three or four priests at Montserrat worked at design constantly. In fact, sketches of a design for one of the private chapels were being sent . . .

Speaking of design, Cloud managed to interject, he was ready to vote for Bak's design of the window with two provisos. The meeting was finally on track. Cloud's two provisos were that Bak work with Michelson and that he make no public statements while the work was in progress. The alternatives, as Cloud saw it, were either a long delay, say ten years, or Albers. Putting off the decision for six months would settle nothing. Bak was not great, but his work showed improvement, and maybe there was little hope for strikingly good work at present.

I asked whether control of Bak's work was possible. The abbot said he thought so. Lancelot expressed concern that Bak might run away with curves. Florian and Cloud agreed that Frei thought Bak's actual work in glass was an improvement over the scale model. Godfrey favored a long delay, six to ten years, rather than settling now for an inferior window.

Discussion see-sawed between Bruno Bak's credibility as an artist and the actual quality of his work. Members began to say how they would vote. Joachim declared he would not vote for Bak; we had heard half a dozen expert opinions on the window and they were all negative. Benedict regarded the choice of Bak as unfortunate from the beginning. He was not an artist of high caliber. A self-respecting artist would have withdrawn after the devastating criticism of his work at our August meeting.

I suggested a secret ballot. Florian wanted an open ballot to identify who voted for the window and who against. All of the committee members would bear responsibility for the outcome, Michael reminded us, and therefore those who were not present—Jeremy was the only one—should be given an opportunity to cast their votes. Godfrey thought we should not vote on either Bak or Albers without the option of voting for a moratorium.

The abbot brought the discussion to a halt by calling for a vote. It was to be a secret ballot on whether or not to have Bak do the window. Slips were distributed and collected by the subprior. He and the abbot counted. The vote was seven yes, four no. Michael wanted the minutes to record that he had voted no. There being no other business, the meeting was adjourned. Jeremy subsequently told the abbot that he would have voted no had he been present.

It's a fair guess that every monk in the community knew the outcome of the vote before lining up for *statio*, the procession into church for Vespers, at 5:30. The underlying issue all along had been, not the artistic quality of the window, but the quality of Bronislaw Bak. Monks liked him, found his personal story moving and the symbolic content of his window appealing. In mid-century everybody was familiar with Pius Parsch's multi-volume commentary on the liturgical seasons, *The Church's Year of Grace*. The Liturgical Press edition went through nine printings between 1953 and 1964. It was easy to interpret the window as symbolizing the year of grace with its intermingled liturgical colors and the great red *sursum corda* reaching up to the source of all grace in Bak's completed design. No wonder there was general agreement in the monastery that the committee had done the right thing.

XIX

What ensued between Marcel Breuer and Abbot Baldwin, however, was a different and more personal story. It only partly came to light at the time and can be appreciated in full now only by reading letters preserved in the abbey archives.

Baldwin did not immediately inform Breuer about the vote. Instead he wrote a letter to Josef Albers on Saturday, November 28, three days after the critical meeting, and sent a copy to Breuer (without noting the copy, it must be said). A week later, December 5, he wrote to Breuer on a different topic, the apse screen.

Breuer had called him some time in the preceding week about progress in selecting an artist to do the screen. The abbot's letter is in response to that call. He apologizes for not writing earlier but says his time has been very much taken up these days. In that connection he says he also wanted to write Breuer personally about the committee's decision in reference to the window, but rather than delay had sent him a carbon of his letter to Albers. Not that he can add much that isn't stated in the letter to Albers. "I believe that you realized the difficulties that confronted us in this decision," he pleads. He credits the committee with coming to the decision only after long deliberation. In view of their long deliberation, he did not feel that he should go contrary to their decision. He has spoken to Mr. Bak at some length and is hopeful that "he will now work more slowly and still improve his sketch and his execution of it."

The rest of the letter concerns the apse screen. He has appointed a subcommittee of four to work out a statement of the subject and suggest artists. They have met several times and have recommended a competition to be announced on the pages of five liturgical art magazines—French, German, Italian, American—if the editors agree. The abbot encloses two copies of the letter to be sent to the editors. He hopes this approach will be acceptable to Breuer. He will be happy to have any further suggestions. He closes with a note that the scaffolding is being removed from the sides of the church. "Now one really gets the full benefit of the beautiful lines, and we are all eagerly waiting for the removal of the scaffolding from the banner."

Baldwin Dworschak was fifty-three years old in 1959. At the beginning of December he was within a few weeks of completing nine years as abbot of a community of Benedictine men that had grown to be the largest in the world during his tenure. He had also been president of Saint John's University until he made the decision to separate the two offices in 1958. As for his character, he was the soul of integrity. He took everything seriously and did everything correctly. He never got sick and he rarely took a vacation. He was an amateur photographer on a modest scale. His interest in piano was nipped in the bud when he came to the Prep School and was told that students were not permitted to play the piano in their first year. It would not be strictly accurate to say he was never seen to relax during his long abbatial tenure. He often strolled with Walter Reger after the evening meal in nice weather, but the quiet warmth and accessibility that characterized him in his long retirement was not much evident between 1950 and 1971.

This is what makes his friendship with Marcel Breuer the more remarkable. That they had become friends in the six years since Breuer first came to Saint John's provides a background for the extraordinary letter that Breuer sent to Baldwin on December 9. He explains that he has just returned from abroad and only received yesterday both the copy of the letter to Albers and the letter addressed to him. He comes to the point immediately: "Your recent decision concerning the north glass wall of the church was a rather sudden blow for me. . . . I should like to document here my feelings in a more definite way than circumstances have required up to now."

What follows is a forceful summary of Breuer's position. He echoes what he had said during the summer about the

architectural function of the window wall. It is an organic part
of the structure. Its particular function will be to control the
light and color of the interior, to set its general atmosphere.
Almost plaintively he adds, "I hate to emphasize the fact, but it
seems that this glass wall belongs to the architect's domain just
as much, or probably more, than to the domain of the artist who
prepares its design." Then as though even this guarded claim
might smack of arrogance, he adds, "at least to a degree that the
architect's opinion should be taken very seriously."

Now he states his opinion: "As the architect of the building, I have to register my conviction that Mr. Bak's window,
though improved since last August, does not have the quali-
ties which I would like to see in the church." The three experts
whom the committee has consulted and its own consultant,
Mr. Kacmarcik, reinforce his feelings. He disclaims intending to
"push the cart of the Albers window," although he says he likes
it and thinks it could be developed into a great contribution to
the church. "But, leaving the matter of the Albers window completely aside, I believe it is better to do nothing than to carry out
the Bak window."

To buttress this categorical dictum, he gives Bak his due:
Bak's first sketch was promising, he has convinced the community that a work can be religious without being figurative,
his intensity and interest are undoubted, he has made improve-
ments since August. All this said, "I still feel that his work is not
good enough for the most important element of the church."
Fans of Bak on the committee were to seize on this character-
ization of the window as proof that Breuer didn't recognize the
ultimate importance of the altar as the major element in any
church. They were less sensitive to his concluding point that "the
integrity of the art work of the church is a moral obligation. Its
importance cannot be overstated."

Transposing the argument to this sphere was expecting a lot
of the committee, perhaps of any committee. Aesthetic integrity was an abstract standard in the best of cases, all the more

so in this case, where there were as yet no works of art to be compared other than the Bak and Albers sketches and an unfinished church interior that was still a forest of metal scaffolding supporting the roof. On a more concrete level, Breuer assured the abbot that he was aware of the feelings that influenced the committee's vote. These feelings were transient and would pass. What was important was "to find some solution for this situation at all costs and all efforts." Mistakes were inevitable in an endeavor of such scale as the building of the church. What was crucial was judgment of the window as a work of art.

Breuer wraps up his letter with a peroration worthy of the rhetorical structure of the whole. "If I reluctantly assume the courage and the role of the critic in such definite terms, I am doing this only because I know that the individual opinions in your own community are divided, and that the consulting outside experts have backed up my stand." He modestly adds that he hopes the abbot will forgive him for "this lengthy declaration" in light of the importance of the problem and concludes "with every good wish to you and the Community."

How Abbot Baldwin would have responded to this letter we can only conjecture because just as he was preparing to reply, he received a second letter from Breuer's office, this one from Ham Smith. Ham's letter was dated December 11 but consisted only of a one-paragraph introduction to a two-page text dated December 7 that he explains he put together "in order that my thinking and reactions on the North Wall would be immediately available to him [Mr. Breuer] on his return." He is sending it now at Mr. Breuer's request in the hope that "it may contribute something to your understanding of the Architect's relation to the total situation."

Unfortunately, Ham's letter seems to have had the opposite effect on Abbot Baldwin. He got it on Monday, December 14, and took both letters to a hastily called meeting of the church planning committee in the monastic lounge at four that afternoon. All but Michael Marx were present. Since there was no convenient way to provide multiple copies of a document on the spur of the moment in 1959, the abbot circulated the Breuer letter to some committee members before the meeting, and he now read Ham's letter to us.

It was well written and perfectly clear. Ham made two points and drew a conclusion. Point number one was that the architect supposed that the proceedings of the summer, the calling in of the two consultants and the meeting with Mr. Bak, were meant to provide a graceful exit for him without requiring a blunt rejection by Mr. Breuer. Point number two was an explanation of how Mr. Bak's design failed to harmonize with the architecture of the church because he did not understand the inner principle of organization that relates all the parts of an artistic work from the smallest to the largest. Following this line of thought, Ham announced his conclusion: Personal feelings must be secondary to what is "essential to the church building": Mr. Bak's commission must be "terminated immediately."

At that point the Breuer ship went down with all hands aboard. The letter sounded like an ultimatum. It lacked both Breuer's large-mindedness and Ham's characteristically judicious understatement. In one unhappy phrase Ham remarked quite accurately that the window, as the largest surface in the church, would create "the basic atmosphere of the church—much more so than the Apse Screen . . . the altars, and any and all other elements combined." To shift metaphors, this was throwing meat to the lions, who pounced on Ham's whole argument because now he was calling the window more important than all the altars in the church!

Of course, that wasn't what he meant, as Breuer would point out in a letter to the abbot on December 18, but this was not the committee's finest hour. Discussion was loose-jointed and random. With something less than complete accuracy, Abbot Baldwin asserted that Breuer had expressed hesitation about Bak's window only on his last visit, and when directly asked whether he would accept or reject Bak, stated that the final choice must be the committee's.

If we had been told earlier what these letters say, the abbot continued, we would have allowed Mr. Breuer to conduct the choice of the window differently. He cannot be expected to realize the consequences for us if we now reject Bak. What the consequences would be he did not say. In the letter he wrote to Breuer the next day, Abbot Baldwin mentioned our commitment to over one hundred persons who had contributed money for individual hexagons, expecting the window to be finished when the church was completed. These donors had most likely been assured that Bak's window was what they were paying for, although that was not said.

The committee's comment was scattered. There were lingering memories of the case against Bak. Bak's window was cold, Albers' warm. The question was not color but design; Bak's design was not good enough for the church. On the contrary, sacred character is what counts, and Bak beats Albers. Temporizing by installing plain glass would make the church a tomb. If we did not want to follow Frank Kacmarcik's advice about the window, we should discharge him. This is the sole reference to Frank in my notes at this juncture, a remarkable absence, since he was everywhere behind the scenes and scathing in his opinion of the committee's final action.

What would the window cost? Alfred asked. Florian estimated $60,000 to $70,000. We would need to go to the Chapter to authorize expenditure for a different window than Bak's. Benedict wondered why that would be necessary when there had been no chapter vote on the $15,000 already spent on glass for the Bak window.

Jeremy said perhaps the one unexpected thing in the whole meeting: we should not go by default. The experts all advised against the Bak window. Therefore, we should not put it in. Abbot Baldwin did not agree. He was not afraid that the window was a great mistake. He questioned Breuer's judgment in this case. He thought Breuer overstated the case for the north wall.

As the meeting was drawing to a close, I suggested that we ask for further clarification of Breuer's letter and invite him to meet with us, but Colman and Florian were not eager for a further meeting. Baldwin said that he understood the committee's sentiments and would not ask for a vote. He would write to Breuer that we stood by our decision. The committee would not discuss the window again.

The abbot wrote to Breuer the next morning. He took exception to the tone of Breuer's letter of December 9. "I was completely unprepared for such a letter as you wrote. . . . The matter of the north window has been under consideration for a long time, and we all assumed that when a final decision would be reached, it would be accepted as such by all."

Despite the uncompromising tone of this opening, he goes on to say, "When your letter reached me, I considered it carefully for a long time and then decided to answer it yesterday morning." What he may have had in mind we can't know. Did he possibly think that the committee's vote should be reconsidered in view of Breuer's strong objection? If he had a soft answer in mind, Smith's letter made backtracking impossible. "But when Mr. Smith's letter of the 11th arrived yesterday morning, I decided to let the committee read both letters and then meet with them." Result: "We do not intend to reverse our decision to let Mr. Bak continue work on the window."

On a more personal note, Baldwin says he is sorry that this situation has occurred, but he doesn't view it with the same alarm as Breuer does, partly because he cannot at all subscribe to Mr. Smith's notion that the window is more important than the "Apse Screen, the altars, and any and all other elements combined." "Not one person here would subscribe to such a statement," he huffs.

"Your letter," he says, "will serve as a record that you did not concur with the client in the matter of the north wall window." We are ready to take full responsibility, he declares, and it is necessary to push ahead with the window because over a hundred donors expect it to be completed at the same time as the church. He ends with appreciation of Breuer's frankness, which cannot have been easy "in the face of a decision already made."

Breuer responded on the 18th with copies to Albers and Kac-marcik. It is a short letter—two paragraphs—and characteristic of the man at his best. If the tone of his letter was not appropri-ate, he wishes to offer a sincere apology. He has appreciated the warmth of his relationship with Saint John's, not a common ex-perience between architect and client. He hopes that the abbot and the community will forgive him for a mistake "of which I was not conscious and which was wholly unintentional."

About the north wall window, he doesn't know that he can add any more to what he has already said. He acknowledges the final decision. He would like to clarify one point, however. When Mr. Smith wrote the offending sentence about the "Apse screen, the altars, and any and all elements combined . . . he was certainly not thinking of the religious significance of those essentials of the church." He has discussed it with Mr. Smith and is quite sure that "he simply meant the purely visual importance of the north window."

Breuer closes "with all good wishes, also to the community." Three days later Abbot Baldwin thanked him for the letter and said the members of the committee would also be grateful for it. "For I know that they were all as eager as I was that our relations remain cordial, and that the full understanding which has existed continue also in the future." He wishes Breuer a blessed Christmas, "also to Mr. Smith."

As Emil Frei had said, most people would find Bak's use of glass charming and like the window very much. Bak and his team had produced a section of forty hexagons to be displayed in the completed hexagon wall. Working through Val Michel-son, and conferring with Bak on site in the old barn, Breuer now offered the artist some general guidelines to bring the com-pleted work into greater artistic harmony with its architectural setting. The planning committee was not part of this process. I understood at the time that Breuer's recommendations generally concerned the scale of the design of individual hexagons and selectively muted colors.

How Bak went about the full-scale drawing and production of all 486 sections of this heroic window is a fascinating story in itself. It is a story that can still be told by Brother Andrew Goltz and Richard Haeg. Andrew took over from a master craftsman temporarily employed by Bak to cut the thousands of pieces of glass in the window through 1960 and spring 1961. Richard first assisted Bak in creating the full-scale drawings laid out on the gym floor or suspended against the section of solid white wall at the northwest corner of the new college dorm, Saint Thomas Aquinas Hall; then did the leading of panel after panel; finally screwed and caulked all 486 panels in place, hexagon by hexagon, in spring and summer of 1961.

January 12–September 1, 1960

XX I have notes on four meetings in 1960, one of them concerned with the organ, the others with sketches for the apse screen and guiding principles for decorating or not decorating the private chapels in the crypt.

On January 12, 1960, the abbot showed some Rucki sketches for artwork in the chapels and spoke of leaving most of the project to Rucki and the Montserrat designers whom he had referred to at an earlier meeting. Cloud was concerned not to overdo decoration. In many of the chapels he recommended simply a "very good crucifix" and two candles attached to the wall rather than placed on the altar. Joachim thought that a few pieces in the abbey collection might be used. He cited Brother Clement Frischauf's Saints Peter and Paul. He suggested naming a jury to approve artworks in the chapels.

The abbot liked this idea. Donors understood that their $5,000 gift did not include a voice in how the chapels were decorated. He asked whether the committee—only Lancelot and Michael were not present—would approve appointing a subcommittee to oversee decorating the private chapels. All but one said yes. The whole committee would get a chance to weigh in on the choice of saints to whom the chapels would be dedicated.

Organ Builders

Without calling for discussion, the abbot mentioned that the estimated cost of the Holtkamp organ was $90,000. He hesitated to ask the Chapter to approve such a large expenditure, but he understood that Holtkamp could build part of the organ now and add to it later. Some members cited the quality of the art and architecture as an argument for not stinting on the organ. Colman urged formation of an organ fund. The meeting adjourned without a resolution.

On March 3 a representative of the organ builder Casavant Frères, a Mr. Northrup, about whom I have no further information, spoke to Abbot Baldwin, Florian, Jerome Coller, and me about doing the church organ. The firm was long established as a leading builder of the classical organ. Mr. Northrup thought that Casavant could build an organ adequate for this church for less than $75,000. They had recently completed an organ of 43 stops, 50 ranks, at Saint Norbert College in Wisconsin. He regarded an organ of 50 ranks as small-scale for our church. Jerome was present to speak for the organists. He focused on use of the organ to accompany monastic processions and chant.

Northrup asked about accompanying the congregation. What was particular about this church was its volume. Of the standard divisions of the organ, he said, in a space of this volume "the Great has to be great." Holtkamp called for two complete choruses in the Great, which was large, and two in the Swell, the only division under expression.

Northrup was not altogether happy about the location of the organ and the console. Casavant had invented electric action. This made it possible to locate the console at some distance from

the wind chests and pipes, but in this church he would prefer
to get the organ works as far forward in the gallery as possible.
He wasn't keen on the spiral metal stairway to the ceiling in the
midst of the ranks of pipes. If there was to be a screen in front of
the organ case, he recommended that it be made of plastic and
recommended a firm that could do this.

Northrup observed that the space for the console was
cramped and deeply recessed, providing room for nothing but a
key desk. This put all the action in the organ case at somewhat
greater expense. Doing it this way favored Holtkamp; Casavant
could make it work; other builders would find it difficult.

As a final word of advice, he remarked that whether we
chose Casavant or some other builder, we would be wise to stick
close to Holtkamp's specifications. There was a little more talk
about particular stops before the abbot asked whether Casavant
could prepare a proposal that would keep the cost of the organ
to about $65,000–$70,000. I do not have further notes about the
organ. It was not discussed again in the committee.

Apse Screen

On June 14 the subcommittee on the design of the apse
screen reported to the full committee. Everybody was present
but Benedict and Michael. We met in SL3, the large classroom
on the first floor of Saint Luke Hall, and looked at some posted
reproductions in the corridor after Cloud showed slides of mosaics by Virgil Cantini and color patterns by Maur van Doors-
laer. Of the artists represented, Godfrey reported that he, Cloud,
and I agreed on a preference for Zach, Baur, and Strawinski.

Alfred asked whether the design needed to be done in
mosaic. To this Cloud said that Breuer suggested mosaic, and
several of the artists contacted said that mosaic would be the
only feasible material for such a large surface. What about doing
it in bronze? someone queried. Whether this would be feasible
Cloud did not know, but he would not like a monochrome work.
Alfred agreed that color was preferable.

The immediate question was whether any of the artists should be invited to present a sketch. The abbot thought that some of them could be eliminated. Kacmarcik should be consulted. Godfrey would have preferred a wider representation and regretted that so few artists had responded to our published notice, but yes, our next step should be to request some artists to submit sketches. What this might cost and whether several artists should be contacted simultaneously concerned Florian. The screen itself, Florian reported, would cost $12,000 to $16,000.

Should Ben Shahn be among the artists invited to submit a sketch? Joachim considered him an outstanding artist who should of course be included on our list, but Abbot Baldwin had reservations. Not only was Shahn not a Catholic, but he was thought to have Communist sympathies. Saint John's could not afford to have the major religious depiction in the church done by anybody with such credentials.

Should we postpone action until hearing Frank's advice and consulting Breuer on his visit next week? There was a certain urgency about moving ahead, if only because the organ builder wanted the artwork on the apse screen in place, or at least simulated before installation of the organ. The abbot finally asked whether there was any objection to proceeding with invitations to the subcommittee's preferred three artists—Baur, Strawinski, and Zach. Since no one objected, he said the names would be submitted to Frank Kacmarcik for his opinion. Cloud said he would like to see sketches by these three, whether or not Frank approved of them. Florian, Godfrey, and John supported him.

The abbot thanked the subcommittee for its efforts, but nothing came of its recommendations. The planning committee did not return to the subject. Unlike the north window-wall, the apse screen could be left blank without conveying the impression that the interior of the church was unfinished. The archives yield some evidence of Abbot Baldwin's continued interest in completing the apse mural according to Breuer's design once the church was in use, but no evidence of a proposal given serious consideration.

Final Meeting

The church planning committee met for the last time on September 1, 1960. Abbot Baldwin called the meeting for 10:45 in the monastery TV room, Abbot Alcuin's old office. The abbot, the subprior, and Benedict, Colman, Florian, Godfrey, Jeremy, Joachim, and I were present. Since we didn't know that this would be our last meeting, there were no concluding remarks, no mutual congratulations and thanks. Breuer and Smith were with us. By now Breuer was working on plans for the monastery and chapel at Mary College in Bismarck and the new library across the mall from the church at Saint John's. He was with the church committee this morning to deal with what must have seemed to him rather secondary questions now that the structure of his great church was complete. The interior was now free of scaffolding. The contractor had notified the architect that he planned to begin bringing woodwork into the building by November 15, implying that laying the brick floor would be completed by then. When should we plan to dedicate the church? Would next May be possible? McGough estimated March 15 as the completion date. What needed to be done before then?

A major point was that the altars in the two large chapels in the crypt be installed as soon as possible so that other work could proceed. What to do about a baldachin over the altar in the parish chapel had yet to be decided. The estimate of $27,000 for a suspended canopy was far too high. Further study was needed.

Stations of the Cross

Upstairs we had yet to decide what to do about Stations of the Cross. Two years ago we had talked about stone tablets set in the floor of the side aisles. Now under consideration was an outdoor-indoor series of four-foot-six-inch concrete pillars bearing wooden crosses, some in the cloister gardens visible from inside the church, others indoors along the north window wall, all of them oriented toward the altar.

Smith was rather fond of this solution, which treated the cloister gardens as interior spaces, but Godfrey thought it was much too fussy and ran counter to the original simplicity of a plan in which even side altars were omitted in order to lend emphasis to the main altar. Smith argued that the short pillars would be seen against large architectural elements—the hexagonal wall, the side-aisle piers—and thus would not seem unduly prominent. Godfrey was not convinced. Colman proposed stational crosses on the window ledges midway between the piers. Arrangements in other churches were cited, one of them clustering all of the stations in one place. This sounded more radical than plaques on the floor. In order to move on, the abbot called for a vote on putting stational plaques on the floor and got a vote of six in favor, two abstaining. If the bishop disapproved, we could do a mock-up of one of the standing stations proposed by Smith and see whether it would do.

Smith presented the drawing of an admirably simple consecration cross, a ten-inch square granite block with a six-inch cross incised in the front and a circular recess on top to hold a sturdy candle on the anniversary of the dedication of the church. Twelve of them were needed to mark the places anointed by the bishop in the dedication ceremony.

Talk about stations and consecration crosses led to considering the glazing of the side windows. From the start Breuer had preferred that these windows be clear glass but had put off a decision in the face of objections, mainly by Godfrey, that looking outdoors would be a distraction from the liturgy. Breuer had stalled, arguing that it would be easier to decide about the clear-glass windows once we experienced the church from inside. We could do that now, and Smith observed that the windows needed to be installed this fall. He added that the architect was assuming that the glazing would be clear glass. No one objected. Should we have screens on the windows? We thought not. Thirty-five years would pass before Abbot Timothy Kelly said yes.

At one point in the meeting Breuer was asked about the traffic square. Would there be a proper approach to the church by the time of the dedication? He replied that it was not in the church contract, but he could proceed with a plan for the area between the library and the church as soon as the library site was definitely settled. The abbot told him that was done. Breuer said that major earth-moving should be done this fall. Smith said that it would be done.

Epilogue

My notes end here. The mall, with its elliptical traffic circle, was done before winter set in. Within six years two Breuer buildings designed to complement the church would rim the mall, Alcuin Library directly across from the church and the science building, now called Peter Engel Hall, beyond faculty parking at the east end.

Inside the church finishing work continued over the winter and well into summer 1961. The major work yet to be completed after the committee's final meeting was fabrication and installation of the north window. Over a period of about a year and a half Bak and his team of young monks and lay workers produced 459 complete hexagons and 54 half hexagons plus a few fractional panels to fill spaces created by the slanting sides of the north wall. Each panel held anywhere from a dozen to thirty pieces of stained glass, no two of the patterns identical. They were stored on wooden racks, then eventually trundled to the church a few at a time, where Richard Haeg, hoisted in an improvised bosun's chair, fixed them in place in the 165-by-65-foot north wall.

With completion of the window, the church was ready to be dedicated. The one large element not in place was the major work of sacred art planned by Breuer for the apse screen. No artist had been found to do the sort of large mosaic he had in mind. In its place a red silk fabric was stretched across the back of the grid to hide the organ works behind it and provide a muted background for the altar and throne.

On August 24 the church was dedicated by Bishop Peter Bartholome. *The Record* covered the event and announced that henceforth all religious services would take place in the new church. I remember how beautiful the church was in the stillness of the evening after the crowd had gone and Marcel Breuer's lighting made the concrete and steel of the banner seem weightless and the granite clefts of the side walls already timeless under the night sky.

Acknowledgments

This book is a personal memoir, not a history. The narrative depends principally on notes I made from meeting to meeting of the planning committee. Nonetheless, I want to acknowledge and thank the archivists of the abbey and the university—David Klingeman, OSB, Brennan Maiers, OSB, and Peggy Roske—for their assistance in pinning down background information on members of the committee and others named in the story. I am particularly grateful for access to the correspondence between Abbot Baldwin Dworschak and Marcel Breuer. Andrew Goltz, OSB, and Richard Haeg provided me with information on how the great north window got built and how it should be read. Monastic confreres of my generation recalled their work as unskilled labor on excavation and formwork in the summer of 1958.

I am indebted to Annette Atkins, Flynn Professor in the Humanities and noted historian, for the distinction between history and memoir, and also to J. P. Earls, OSB, Al Eisele, Eric Hollas, OSB, and Tom Joyce, for their generous comments and suggestions at various points along the way. Professor Renée Cheng, head of the School of Architecture at the University of Minnesota, kindly provided just the kind of illustrations I wanted in the book from her portfolio of pen sketches. Victoria Young, associate professor of architectural history at the University of Saint Thomas in Saint Paul, read an early draft of the manuscript and encouraged me to publish it in time for the fiftieth anniversary of the dedication of the church. Her forthcoming book on the church will provide a definitive account of its design, construction, and architectural significance. An in-house record of the stages of construction can be found in the *Scriptorium* for 1961 in an article by Brian Millette, OSB, "St. John's New Abbey Church: A Chronicle of Construction."

Roster of Names

Josef Albers. Artist. (1888–1976)

Lancelot Atsch, OSB. Collegeville pastor. (1909–1986)

Benedict Avery, OSB. College: Classics. (1919–2008)

Bronislaw Bak. Stained glass artist. (1922–1981)

Colman Barry, OSB. College: History. (1921–1994)

Marcel Breuer. Architect. (1902–1981)

Doris Caesar. Expressionist sculptor. (1892–1971)

Hubert Dahlheimer, OSB. Saint Joseph pastor. (1906–1992)

Alfred Deutsch, OSB. College: English. (1914–1989)

Godfrey Diekmann, OSB. *Orate Fratres* editor. (1908–2002)

Isabelle Durenberger. Alumni secretary, development.
    (1911–2008)

Baldwin Dworschak, OSB. Abbot. (1906–1996)

Richard Eckroth, OSB. Brother master. (1926–)

John Eidenschink, OSB. Subprior. (1914–2004)

Gerard Farrell, OSB. Organist. (1919–2000)

Emil Frei Jr. Stained glass consultant. (1896–1967)

Robert Gatje. Breuer associate. (1927–)

Andrew Goltz, OSB. Stained glass artisan. (1933–)

Arno Gustin, OSB. SJU dean, president. (1906–1991)

Richard Haeg. Stained glass artisan. (1933–)

Ray Hermanson. Local architect. (1916–2003)

Walter Holtkamp. Organ builder. (1894–1962)

Frank Kacmarcik. Art consultant. (1920–2004)

Malcolm Lein. Architect consultant. (1913–)

Michael Marx, OSB. Seminary: Theology. (1913–1993)

Charles McGough. Contractor. (1919–2000)

Gerald McMahon, OSB. College: Religion. (1901–1976)

Cloud Meinberg, OSB. College: Art, architecture. (1914–1982)

Val Michelson. Architect supervisor on site. (1916–2006)

Florian Muggli, OSB. Treasurer. (1925–2010)

Jeremy Murphy, OSB. College: Political Science. (1908–1985)

Walter Reger, OSB. College: History; alumni director.
    (1894–1971)

William Saltzman. Artist consultant. (1916–2006)

Hamilton Smith. Breuer associate. (1925–)

Hilary Thimmesh, OSB. College: English. (1928–)

Joachim Watrin, OSB. Prep School: Geometry. (1906–1983)